PRAYERS

FOR

CALM

PRAYERS
FOR
CALM

Meditations,
Affirmations, and
Prayers to Soothe
Your Soul

By BECCA ANDERSON

CORAL GABLES

Published by Mango Publishing Group, a division of Mango Media Inc.

Cover, Layout & Design: Morgane Leoni

For permission requests, please contact the publisher at:
Mango Publishing Group
2850 S Douglas Road, 2nd Floor
Coral Gables, FL 33134 USA
info@mango.bz

For special orders, quantity sales, course adoptions and corporate sales, please email the publisher at sales@mango.bz. For trade and wholesale sales, please contact Ingram Publisher Services at customer.service@ingramcontent.com or +1.800.509.4887.

Prayers for Calm: Meditations, Affirmations, and Prayers to Soothe Your Soul

Library of Congress Cataloging-in-Publication number: 2019944227
ISBN: (print) 978-1-63353-992-1, (ebook) 978-1-63353-993-8
BISAC category code EL087000, RELIGION / Prayer

Printed in the United States of America

For Richard Jin Chin, the kindest man in the world.
Love eternal

Trust the bend in the road.

—ruth weiss

CONTENTS

INTRODUCTION Add Meaning to Your Life Every Day with Prayer   8

JANUARY Reassurances for Uncertain Times   11

FEBRUARY You Are Not Alone: Affirmations of Love and Support   31

MARCH Serenity Prayers   52

APRIL Springing Back from Anything   71

MAY Blooming Under Pressure   93

JUNE Blessings for When You're Stressing   116

JULY Staying Calm When Anxiety Strikes   140

AUGUST Meditations for Moving Forward   165

SEPTEMBER Finding the Stillness Within   190

OCTOBER Calming Contemplations   212

NOVEMBER Attitudes of Gratitude   233

DECEMBER Comfort and Joy: Looking Ahead to a New Year Reset   251

ABOUT THE AUTHOR   276

Add Meaning to Your Life Every Day with Prayer

I once had the pleasure of attending a talk by Huston Smith, a preeminent scholar of the world's religions who first came to the attention of the world when he brought a young Tibetan Buddhist monk—His Holiness, the Dalai Lama—to America for the first time. Smith spoke about the continuing impact of spirituality in our world, most notably on the strife in the Middle East over religious differences. He was at his most joyous when he spoke about his own spiritual practices, which he described to us. They were beautiful in their simplicity. Smith said that, upon rising each day, he did Hatha yoga for some minutes, followed by reading a few pages of sacred text, after which he meditated or prayed for at least five minutes. He would finish his morning ritual by doing a bit of yard work and some composting, which resulted in rich, dark soil and a beautiful garden.

The entire audience smiled raptly as they listened to this great and humble man describe the simple spiritual practices with which he began each day. These were Huston Smith's personal morning rituals. I loved the irony that this premier academic, who has such a deep understanding of all the religious rituals throughout history, had created such an uncomplicated practice for himself. I left the talk inspired and soon felt compelled to write a book of rituals that add meaning into our lives.

9

Whether people are conscious of it or not, our lives are centered upon rituals such as prayer. The weekly Wednesday night pizza and movie with the kids is a family ritual. It could be greatly enriched by adding a spiritual aspect—perhaps children could share the highlight of their week so far, and photos or memories could be added to a family album to be treasured for generations to come. The Saturday night date is a romantic ritual, knitting circles are a growing trend, and doing yoga is replacing going to the gym as a spiritual and physical workout. People need ritual to inform and enrich their lives, to deal with stress, and above all, to create meaning in their lives.

Together with seasonal rituals, daily spiritual practices such as prayer and meditation create a life filled with blessings. Many of us were brought up with specific religious practices. Although I was brought up as a First Day Adventist, when I studied history, I kept discovering practices from the past that I felt were just as relevant today. One ancient ritual I discovered was bibliomancy, which is a form of divination developed when books were precious objects made of papyrus or vellum. Bibliomancy is a simple ritual that I have incorporated into my daily life for inspiration "from the gods." You simply open a book at random and let a word or phrase come to your attention. You thus become inspired in the true meaning of the word: simply to breathe in. I hope you can use this book in this way, for instant inspiration, to find a meditation in a moment, or, most of all, to find a place of calm and serenity you can turn to anytime you need it.

JANUARY

REASSURANCES FOR UNCERTAIN TIMES

You alone are enough. You have nothing to prove to anybody."

   —*Maya Angelou*

"Faith is taking the first step even when you don't see the whole staircase."

   —*Martin Luther King Jr.*

"The Lord bless you and keep you; The Lord make his face shine upon you and be gracious to you; The Lord turn his face toward you and give you peace."

   —*Numbers 6:24-26*

"Do not lose hope, please believe that there are a thousand beautiful things waiting for you. Sunshine comes to all who feel rain."

   —*R. M. Drake*

"God does not send us despair in order to kill us; he sends it in order to awaken us to new life."

   —*Hermann Hesse*

— 1 —

WE ARE BRANCHES OF THE SAME TREE

All human beings are limbs of each other,
having been created of one essence.

When time affects a limb with pain,
The other limbs cannot at rest remain.
If thou feel not other's misery,

A human being is no name for thee.
—Sa'adi, 1210–1290

— 2 —

TAKE POSITIVE ACTION

In a time of destruction, create something.
A poem.
A parade.
A community.
A school.
A vow.
A moral principle.
One peaceful moment.
—Maxine Hong Kingston

13

— 3 —

EVERYTHING WILL BE ALL RIGHT

I will breathe.
I will think of solutions.
I will not let my worry control me.
I will not let my stress level break me.
I will simply breathe.
And it will be okay.
Because I don't quit.
– Shayne McClendon

— 4 —

STILL I RISE

You will become a graveyard
of all the women you once were
before you rise one morning
embraced by your own skin.
You will swallow a thousand
different names
before you taste the meaning
held within your own.
–Pavana

— 5 —

THE SOUL WALKS ALL PATHS

The hidden well-spring of your soul must needs
rise and run murmuring to the sea;
And the treasure of your infinite depths
would be revealed to your eyes.
But let there be no scales to weigh your unknown treasure;
And seek not the depths of your knowledge
with staff or sounding line.
For self is a sea boundless and measureless.
Say not, "I have found the truth,"
but rather, "I have found a truth."
Say not, "I have found the path of the soul."
Say rather, "I have met the soul walking upon my path."
For the soul walks upon all paths.
The soul walks not upon a line, neither does it grow like a reed.
The soul unfolds itself, like a lotus of countless petals.
–Kahlil Gibran

— 6 —

YOU ARE BRAVE

I am whole.
I am learning.
I am letting go.
I am free.
I am talented and courageous.
I am protecting my joy.

15

I am brave.
I am healing.
I am loving myself.
Unapologetically.
–Alex Elle

— 7 —

DO NOT DESPAIR

Let no sadness come to this heart.
Let not trouble come to these arms.
Let no conflict come to these eyes.
Let my soul be filled
with the blessing of joy and peace.
–Hamsa Prayer

— 8 —

RESPECT YOURSELF

Learn to be alone
without being lonely.
Learn to admire your beauty
without finding fault.
Learn to love yourself
without the love of others.
–h.r.d.

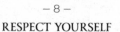

— 9 —

I WILL NOT DIE AN UNLIVED LIFE

I will not die an unlived life.
I will not live in fear of falling or catching fire.
I choose to inhabit my days,
to allow my living to open me,
to make me less afraid,
more accessible,
to loosen my heart
until it becomes a wing.
—Dawna Markova

— 10 —

LIVE THE LIFE YOU ALWAYS IMAGINED

I learned this, at least
by my experiment:
that if one advances confidently
in the direction of his dreams,
and endeavors to live the life
which he has imagined,
he will meet with a success
unexpected in common hours.
—Henry David Thoreau, Walden, 1854

— 11 —

LIKE A BRIDGE OVER TROUBLED WATER

When trouble is close at hand.
Your Word will be a lamp for me,
a guide to light my way,
a solid place to set my feet,
a compass when I stray.

May I live my life to praise You,
not for fortune, nor for fame,
may everything I say and do
bring glory to Your name.

May my eyes stay fixed upon You
as I seek the way that's pure,
tasting Your love and goodness
sleeping and rising secure.

Planted by Your living streams
I'll delight in all Your ways,
hidden by Your sheltering wings
with new mercies for each day.

Even in a dangerous land
when storms threaten to destroy,
at the cross I'll stand upon the Rock
my Strength, my Hope, my Joy.

Dear Lord, show me Your favor,
at all times keep me blessed,

may Your face ever shine upon me,
with peace and perfect rest. Amen.
—Mary Fairchild

— 12 —

STRONGER THAN THE STORM WITHIN ME

I will trust in the
darkness and know that my
times, even now, are in Your
hand. Tune my spirit to the
music of heaven, and
somehow, make my
obedience count for You.
—The Prayer of Saint Brendan

— 13 —

FIND REFUGE HERE

He will cover you with his feathers,
and under his wings you will find refuge;
his faithfulness will be your shield and rampart.
You will not fear the terror of night,
nor the arrow that flies by day,

nor the pestilence that stalks in the darkness,
nor the plague that destroys at midday.
—Psalm 91:1–16

— 14 —

LIVE WITH AN OPEN HEART

Dance, when you're broken open.
Dance, if you've torn the bandage off.
Dance in the middle of the fighting.
Dance in your blood.
Dance, when you're perfectly free.
—Rumi, 13th century Persian poet

— 15 —

FRET NOT

Don't worry,
be happy!
—Meher Baba

— 16 —

BECOMING YOUR BEST YOU

Close your eyes
and imagine the best

version of you possible.
That's who you really are.
Let go of any part of you
that doesn't believe it.
—C. Assaid

— 17 —

TAKE TIME TO HEAL

To everything there is a season,
a time for every purpose under the sun.
A time to be born and a time to die;
a time to plant and a time to pluck up that which is planted;
a time to kill and a time to heal...
a time to weep and a time to laugh;
a time to mourn and a time to dance...
a time to embrace and a time to refrain from embracing;
a time to lose and a time to seek;
a time to rend and a time to sew;
a time to keep silent and a time to speak;
a time to love and a time to hate;
a time for war and a time for peace.
—Ecclesiastes 3:1-8

— 18 —

YOU'RE BRAVER THAN YOU KNOW

Promise me you'll always remember:
you're braver than you believe,
and stronger than you seem,
and smarter than you think.
–Christopher Robin to Pooh, A.A. Milne

— 19 —

WHAT YOU CAN RISE FROM

You may encounter many defeats,
but you must not be defeated.
In fact, it may be necessary to encounter the defeats,
so you can know who you are,
what you can rise from,
how you can still come out of it.
–Maya Angelou

— 20 —

WISDOM UNTANGLES THE MIND

The Tao is wisdom eternally inexhaustible.
Fathomless for the mere intellect,
The Tao is the law wherewith all things come into being.

It blunts the edges of the intellect,
Untangles the knots of the mind,

Softens the glare of thinking,
And settles the dust of thought.

Transparent yet invisible,
The Tao exists like deep pellucid water.
Its origin is unknown,
For it existed before Heaven and Earth
—Lao Tsu

— 21 —

FINDING CONTENTMENT IN EVERY SITUATION

I know what it is to be in need,
and I know what it is to have plenty.
I have learned the secret of being content
in any and every situation,
whether well fed or hungry,
whether living in plenty or in want.
I can do all this through him who gives me strength.
—Philippians 4:12-13

— 22 —

SHINE YOUR LIGHT AND SHARE YOUR LIGHT

Thousands of candles
can be lit from a single candle,
and the life of the candle

will not be shortened.
Happiness never decreases by being shared.
–Buddha

— 23 —

HAPPY IS THE PERSON WHO DOES WHAT IS RIGHT

Doing the right thing is our best gift;
That is what brings us bliss and happiness.
Happy and blissful is the person who does what is right,
because it is the right thing to do.
–Vohu Prayer

— 24 —

TAKE THE LESSON IN EVERYTHING THAT HAPPENS

And even in our sleep,
pain that cannot forget
falls drop by drop upon the heart,
and in our own despair,
against our will,
comes wisdom to us
by the awful grace of God.
–Aeschylus

— 25 —

KNOW THERE IS LOVE IN THE WORLD

At the center of the universe is a
loving heart that continues to beat
and that wants the best for every person.

Anything we can do to help foster
the intellect and spirit and emotional growth
of our fellow human beings, that is our job.

Those of us who have this particular vision
must continue against all odds.

Life is for service.
–Fred Rogers, *Mr. Rogers' Neighborhood*

— 26 —

HAVE A COMPASSIONATE HEART

Be kind,
for everyone
you meet
is carrying
a great
burden.
–Ian Maclaren, 1898

— 27 —

SINK INTO JOY

Flowers, sesame-seed, bowls of fresh water, a tuft of kusha grass,
all this altar paraphernalia is not needed
by someone who takes the teacher's words in
and honestly lives them.

Full of longing in meditation,
one sinks into a joy that is free of any impulse to act,
and will never enter a human birth again.
—Lalia, 1381

— 28 —

LIFE IS NOT FOR THE FAINT OF HEART

Fearlessness is better
than a faint heart
for any man who puts
his nose out of doors.
The length of my life and the day
of my death were fated long ago.
—Ancient Norse Verse

— 29 —

IT'S OK TO BE VULNERABLE

Don't worry, it's going to be OK.
It's all right, little one, you're safe and loved.

It's OK to cry, it's OK to be afraid, it's OK to be weak,
it's OK to be vulnerable, it's OK to be human.

It's from all these elements that we grow,
and it's from all these elements that I am born out of you.

I Love You.

You're not alone.
So long as you reach out to others, you're never alone.
Ask for my help in loaning you the courage you already have.
It's not that I never give you more than you can handle,
I am not responsible for the consequences of your actions,
only you are.

Stay on the path if you're suffering
by taking the steps you need to take.
Hang on and hang in there, because it's now
that you're growing at light speed.
You're never going backward, only forward.

—Anonymous

— 30 —

DON'T FORGET TO COLOR OUTSIDE THE LINES

Your attitude is
like a box of crayons
that color your world.

—Allen Klein

27

— 31 —

PUT ASIDE ALL ANXIOUS THOUGHTS

Do not look forward to what may happen
tomorrow; the same everlasting Father who cares
for you today will take care of you tomorrow and
every day. Either He will shield you from suffering,
or He will give you unfailing strength to bear it.
Be at peace, then. Put aside all anxious thoughts and
imaginations, and say continually:
"The Lord is my strength and my shield.
My heart has trusted in Him and I am helped.
He is not only with me but in me,
and I in Him."
—St. Francis de Sales

DEVOTIONS FOR DOWN DAYS

"It is okay to be at a place of struggle. Struggle is just another word for growth."
—*Neale Donald Walsch*

"Problems are not stop signs; they are guidelines."
—*Robert Schuller*

"Be patient. Sometimes you have to go through the worst to get to the best. Give time some time."
—*Karen Salmansohn*

"Patience is the calm acceptance that things can happen in a different order than the one you have in mind."
—*David G. Allen*

"Maturity of mind is the capacity to endure uncertainty."
—*John Huston Finley*

PRAYERFUL PRACTICE

Every Breath Is a Blessing: Breath-Focused
Meditation (1–5 Minutes)

The breath-focused meditation is typically a short meditation intended to refocus you during your day. You can do this anytime, anywhere. I usually do it when I feel particularly stressed but don't have a lot of time to meditate.

Start by sitting in a comfortable position. Take a deep breath in and let it go, slowly, gently closing your eyes, then return to breathing normally. Take a few moments to notice how your body feels. Does it feel good? Are you sore anywhere? Once you've acknowledged these feelings, allow yourself to let them go. Softly pull your focus inward to your breaths. Notice how each intake of air is different from the last. If you find yourself straying to other thoughts, gently let go of them, allow them to pass you by, and bring yourself back to the breath. Allow your breath to lead your mind instead of the other way around. Continue this for a few moments. When you're ready, slowly, gently open your eyes. Think of the blessings in your life and continue your day with that sense of being blessed.

FEBRUARY

YOU ARE NOT ALONE: AFFIRMATIONS OF LOVE AND SUPPORT

Crying does not indicate that you are weak.
Since birth, it has always been a sign that you
are alive."
　—*Charlotte Bronte*

"Trust in him at all times, O people; pour out your
heart before him; God is a refuge for us."
　—*Psalm 62:8*

"So many people love you. Don't focus on the
people who don't."
　—*Colin Tate*

"It is part of the
human experience to feel pain
do not be afraid
open yourself to it."
　—*Rupi Kaur, evolving*

"Everything in moderation,
including moderation."
　—*Anonymous*

— 1 —

THE OPTIMIST'S CREED

To be so strong that nothing
can disturb your peace of mind.

To talk health, happiness, and prosperity
to every person you meet.

To make all your friends feel
that there is something in them.

To look at the sunny side of everything
and make your optimism come true.

To think only the best, to work only for the best,
and to expect only the best.

To be just as enthusiastic about the success of others
as you are about your own.

To forget the mistakes of the past
and press on to the greater achievements of the future.

To wear a cheerful countenance at all times
and give every living creature you meet a smile.

To give so much time to the improvement of yourself
that you have no time to criticize others.

To be too large for worry, too noble for anger, too strong for fear,
and too happy to permit the presence of trouble.

To think well of yourself and to proclaim this fact to the world,
not in loud words but great deeds.

To live in faith that the whole world is on your side
so long as you are true to the best that is in you.
–Christian D. Larson, 1912

– 2 –

HAPPINESS IS WORTH STRIVING FOR

You are a child of the universe,
no less than the trees and the stars;
you have a right to be here.
And whether or not it is clear to you,
no doubt the universe is unfolding as it should.

Therefore be at peace with God,
whatever you conceive Him to be,
and whatever your labors and aspirations,
in the noisy confusion of life keep peace with your soul.

With all its sham, drudgery, and broken dreams,
it is still a beautiful world.
Be cheerful.
Strive to be happy.
–Max Ehrmann, 1927

— 3 —

WITH DEEP PRAYER COMES DEEP PEACE

Pray for what you cannot see.
Pray clearly
for what you can only faintly grasp.
Pray silently
from the core of your being.
Pray for healing.
Pray for humanity.

Pray lovingly
Pray deeply–
pray so deeply that
the prayer and the praying
become one.
–Charlie Elkind

— 4 —

KNOW THAT YOU ARE NOT ALONE

All you who sleep tonight
Far from the ones you love,
No hand to left or right,
And emptiness above–
Know that you aren't alone.
The whole world shares your tears,
Some for two nights or one,
And some for all their years.
–Vikram Seth

— 5 —

YOU WON'T FEEL THIS WAY FOREVER

That's how you stay alive.
When it hurts so much you can't breathe,
that's how you survive.
By remembering that,
one day, somehow, impossibly,
you won't feel this way.
It won't hurt this much.
—Grey's Anatomy

— 6 —

ETERNAL LOVE FOR ALL IN THE WORLD

For as long as space endures
And for as long as living beings remain
Until then may I too abide
To dispel the misery of the world.
—Shantideva

— 7 —

LET THAT WORD BE: THANKS

Better
than if there were thousands

of meaningless words is
one
meaningful
word
that on hearing
brings peace.

Better
than if there were thousands
of meaningless verses is
one
meaningful
verse
that on hearing
brings peace.

And better than chanting hundreds
of meaningless verses is
one
Dhamma-saying
that on hearing
brings peace.

—Dhammapada, VIIIii, attributed to Buddha

— 8 —

ALL THINGS MUST PASS

Let nothing disturb you.
Let nothing frighten you.

All things are passing away;
God never changes.
Patience obtains all things.
Whoever has God lacks nothing;
God alone suffices.
–Saint Teresa of Avila

– 9 –

TOWARD HEAVEN

Refuse to fall down.
If you cannot refuse to fall down,
refuse to stay down.
If you cannot refuse to stay down,
lift your heart toward heaven
and like a hungry beggar,
ask that it be filled,
and it will be filled.
You may be pushed down.
You may be kept from rising.
But no one can keep you
from lifting your heart
toward heaven–
only you.
It is in the midst of misery
that so much becomes clear.

The one who says nothing good
came of this,
is not yet listening.
−Clarissa Pinkola Estes

− 10 −

THE GREATEST TRUTH OF LOVE

don't be afraid
of what you do not understand
and cannot yet grasp
if you are lost
in the dark night of the soul
nothing has ever happened
that was not meant
even if your thoughts
tell you this is not so

we share the same intertwined heaven
we are carried and held in the same light
we are loved in the same light
light will not elude you

let every breath
fill your mind with peace
let your soul unfold courageously
in divine wisdom
and open itself for the beautiful things
that want to enter your life from the future

the greatest truth of love
the only thing that matters
is that you are alive.
–Swedish Chant

— 11 —

A GUIDE FOR THOSE WHO HAVE LOST THEIR WAY

May I become at all times, both now and forever
A protector for those without protection
A guide for those who have lost their way
A ship for those with oceans to cross
A bridge for those with rivers to cross
A sanctuary for those in danger
A lamp for those without light
A place of refuge for those who lack shelter
And a servant to all in need.
–Buddhist Prayer of Peace

— 12 —

ONLY CONNECT

A thousand fibers connect us
with our fellow men;
and among those fibers,
as sympathetic threads,

our actions run as causes,
and they come back to us as effects.
—Herman Melville

— 13 —

WE ARE ON THE SAME PATH

Religions are different roads
converging upon the same point.
What does it matter
that we take different roads
so long as we reach the same goal.
—Mahatma Gandhi

— 14 —

FOR EVERY CARE, A PROMISE

May God give you
For every storm, a rainbow
For each tear, a smile
For every care, a promise
And a blessing in each trial.
A faithful friend to share,
For every sigh, a sweet song,
And an answer for each prayer.
May the blessing of God's soft rain be on you.
—From Irish Oral Tradition

41

— 15 —

THE BUDDHA'S GUIDE TO GRATITUDE

Give thanks
For what has been given to you,
However little.
Be pure, never falter.

—Buddha

— 16 —

SEEK AND YE SHALL FIND

Ask, and it shall be given you;
Seek, and you shall find;
Knock, and it shall be opened to you.
For whoever asks, receives;
And he who seeks, finds;
And to him who knocks, the door is opened.

—Matthew 7:7

— 17 —

ALL LIFE IS BOUND TOGETHER

Humankind has not woven the web of life.
We are but one thread within it.
Whatever we do to the web,

we do to ourselves.
All things are bound together.
All things connect.
–Chief Seattle

— 18 —

YOU WILL NEVER BE FORSAKEN

Be strong and courageous.
Do not be afraid or terrified,
for the LORD your God goes with you;
he will never leave you nor forsake you.
–Deuteronomy 31:6

— 19 —

THE TAO OF NOW

The Tao that can be told
is not the eternal Tao.
The name that can be named
is not the eternal Name.

The unnamable is the eternally real.
Naming is the origin
of all particular things.

Free from desire, you realize the mystery.
Caught in desire, you see only the manifestations.

43

Yet mystery and manifestations
arise from the same source.
This source is called darkness.

Darkness within darkness.
The gateway to all understanding.
—Lao Tse

— 20 —

WHAT GOD SOWS IN THE HEART

Give over thine own willing;
give over thine own running;
give over thine own desiring
to know or to be anything;
and let that grow in thee,
and be in thee,
and breathe in thee,
and act in thee,
and thou shalt find by sweet experience
that the Lord knows that,
and loves and owns that,
and will lead it to
the inheritance of life,
which is its portion.
—Isaac Pennington, 1661

— 21 —

HOW TO BE HAPPY IN THE HERE AND NOW

There is no way to happiness,
happiness is the way.

You should be happy right in the here and now.
There is no way to enlightenment.
Enlightenment should be right here and right now.
The moment when you come back to
yourself, mind and body together,
fully present, fully alive, that is already enlightenment.
You are no longer a sleepwalker.
You are no longer in a dream.
You are fully alive.
You are awake.
Enlightenment is there.

And if you continue each moment like that,
enlightenment becomes deeper.
More powerful.

There is no way to enlightenment,
enlightenment is the way.
–Thích Nhất Hạnh

— 22 —

REACH OUT

No act of kindness, no matter how small, is ever wasted.
–Aesop

— 23 —

MAKE USE OF EACH PRECIOUS DAY

This life, you must know
as the tiny splash of a raindrop:

A thing of beauty that disappears as it comes into being.

Therefore, set your goal.
Make use of every day and every night.
—Tsongkhapa

— 24 —

DON'T WAIT. BE HERE NOW.

There is only one time
when it is essential to awaken.
That time is now.
—Jack Kornfield

— 25 —

LEARN TO LOOK AT YOURSELF

Love means to learn to look at yourself
The way one looks at distant things
For you are only one thing among many.

And whoever sees that way heals his heart,
Without knowing it, from various ills
—Czeslaw Milosz

— 26 —

GOD IS WITHIN US ALL

May all I say and all I think
be in harmony with Thee,
God within me, God beyond me,
Maker of the Trees.
—Chinook Chant, Native North American

— 27 —

ENTER INTO SOUL LIGHT

Step into the Sunlight
Feel the pain wash away
Enter in the Soul-light
Just BE in today.

Forget all emotion
Put your trust in the day
Let the past rush on by you
Put your Self in THE WAY.
—Lynne Milum

47

– 28 –

YOUR LIFE IS A PRAYER

When I am liberated by silence,
when I am no longer involved
in the measurement of life, but in the living of it,
I can discover a form of prayer in which
there is effectively no distraction.
My whole life becomes a prayer.
My whole silence is full of prayer.
The world of silence in which I am immersed
contributes to my prayer.

–Thomas Merton

LIVE WITH YOUR HEART WIDE OPEN TO LOVE

"All I ever wanted was to reach out and touch another human being, not just with my hands, but with my heart."
—*Tahereh Mafi*

"The Lord your God is with you, the Mighty Warrior who saves. He will take great delight in you; in his love, he will no longer rebuke you, but will rejoice over you with singing."
—*Zephaniah 3:17*

"Let yourself be silently drawn by the strange pull of what you really love. It will not lead you astray."
—*Rumi*

"The greatest thing in the world is to know how to belong to oneself."
—*Michel de Montaigne*

"The only time we waste is the time we spend thinking we are alone."
—*Mitch Albom*

SELF-CARE STRATEGIES FOR A STRESSFUL WORLD

My daily practice goes something like this. Almost without exception, I meditate daily. Most days I meditate for twenty minutes, sometimes less, sometimes more. The important thing for me is to do it daily. Consistency is key. I believe making meditation a daily habit trumps duration of time sitting in silence. Later, after tea and other self-care practices, I take a mindful walk with my dog. Pets can be a great contribution to a mindful life. For me, I have found having a dog helps me to be more consistent in my focus and mindful of the time passing during the day. Dogs live mindfully and in tune with nature! All animals live mindfully, for they only know the present moment. Although they sometimes eat too quickly, they know when they are hungry and they let us know. Many people believe they are too busy to care for an animal. I would say this might be exactly the reason to get one. Pets force us to slow down. They motivate us to walk and spend time in nature. I often listen to podcasts while walking my dog. However, I try to walk at least three times a week in silence, taking in the world around me with my senses. I smell the scents around me on my mindful walk. I feel my feet hitting the ground, and I notice my body and how it moves in space. I look at the light and see all the colors around me. I sometimes even try to taste the air, if it is pleasant. The more one taps into the senses, the more present we become.

Animals also teach us about compassion. They love unconditionally. Have you noticed that it is hard to live in the moment and be self-critical? Compassion and curiosity are essential factors of living in the moment. If I find myself upset, frustrated, or angry, I slow down and try to process. I may try some gentle or restorative yoga, especially on days when there is a lot to sort out. If I feel particularly overwhelmed, I sit down and meditate again. Another daily practice that calms my body and centers my mind is abhyanga, a mindful practice based in Ayurveda that means self-massage. In traditional abhyanga, one uses oil, such as sesame or coconut oil, sometimes infused with essential oils. Abhyanga can be as simple as massaging your own hands or feet or the entire body. The importance of abhyanga comes from its link to compassion. When we treat ourselves kindly, the rewards are great. I find that abhyanga helps me to be more self-reliant and proactive. I am taking care of myself through my own sense of loving touch and mindful self-care. When I care for myself with my own hands, I take time to reflect on the sacredness and importance of myself right now. I pay careful attention and am mindful of my own body and health. This is one of my favorite mindful practices.

MARCH

SERENITY PRAYERS

"If it costs you your peace, it's too expensive."
  —*Unknown*

"It is impossible to feel grateful and depressed in the same moment."
  —*Naomi Williams*

"Calm me, Lord, as you calmed the storm. Still me, Lord, keep me from harm. Let all tumult within me cease. Enfold me, Lord, in your peace."
  —*Celtic prayer*

"I have said these things to you that in me you may have peace. In the world, you will have tribulation. But take heart; I have overcome the world."
  —*John 16:33*

53

"One day at a time, one step at a time, and you'll get there."
  —*Bill W.*

— 1 —

ENGAGE

Respond; don't react.
Listen; don't talk.
Think; don't assume.
–Raji Lukkoor

— 2 —

THE SERENITY PRAYER

God, grant me serenity to accept the things I cannot change,
Courage to change the things I can,
and wisdom to know the difference.
–Reinhold Niebuhr

— 3 —

ONE MOMENT AT A TIME

Living one day at a time;
enjoying one moment at a time;
accepting hardship as the pathway to peace.
Taking, as He did,
this sinful world as it is,
not as I would have it;

trusting that He will make all things right if
I surrender to His will;
that I may be reasonably happy in this life
and supremely happy with Him forever in the next. Amen.
—William Hutchison Murray

— 4 —

NO LINE

When someone is full of Love and Compassion,
he cannot draw a line between
two countries, two faiths, or two religions.

—Amma

— 5 —

READ YOUR OWN HEART RIGHT

We would have inward peace,
Yet will not look within;
We would have misery cease,
Yet will not cease from sin;

Once, read your own heart right
And you will have done with fears;
Man gets no other light
Though he search a thousand years.
—Matthew Arnold, 1852

— 6 —

QUIET YOUR MIND

When I had no friend, I made
Quiet my friend. When I had no
Enemy, I opposed my body.

When I had no temple, I made
My voice my temple. I have
No priest, my tongue is my choir.

When I have no means, fortune
Is my means. When I have
Nothing, death will be my fortune.

Need is my tactic, detachment
Is my strategy. When I had
No lover, I courted my sleep.
—Robert Pinsky

— 7 —

SONGS IN THE NIGHT

Come, Spirit,
make me docile to your voice.
Help me debate angels.
Let your will be done in me
even if it means

misunderstanding,

rejection,

scandal.

Give me wisdom to find you

in the irrational:

heavens gone awry,

astrologers' predictions,

Give me such hospitality of heart that

songs in the night.

family,

foreign seers,

poor shepherds and animals

find a home in my presence.

—Benedictine Sisters, Living in Peace

– 8 –

THE HEALING POWER OF BEAUTY

Today, like every other day,

we wake up empty and frightened.

Don't open the door to the study and begin reading.

Take down a musical instrument.

Let the beauty we love be what we do.

There are hundreds of ways to kneel and kiss the ground.

—Rumi, 13th century Persian poet

— 9 —

GIFTS OF GRACE

Sometimes we may ask God for success,
and He gives us physical and mental stamina.
We might plead for prosperity,
and we receive enlarged perspective
and increased patience,
or we petition for growth
and are blessed with the gift of grace.
He may bestow upon us conviction and confidence
as we strive to achieve worthy goals.
–David A. Bednar

— 10 —

TRY LOOKING AT THINGS A DIFFERENT WAY

Mindfulness: taking a balanced approach to negative
emotions so that feelings are neither suppressed nor
exaggerated. We cannot ignore our pain and feel compassion
for it at the same time. Mindfulness requires that we
not "over-identify" with thoughts and feelings so that
we are caught up and swept away by negativity.
–Brené Brown

— 11 —

DEEP REST

May the gentleness of God's supportive
and sustaining love
gather us in her arms this day/night,
and bless us with sleep that restores both body and soul. Amen.
—**Marchiene Vroon Rienstra**

— 12 —

KEEP SERENITY IN YOUR HEART

While you are proclaiming peace
with your lips,
be careful to have it
even more fully in your heart.
—**St. Francis of Assisi**

— 13 —

KEEP CALM AND CARRY ON

You can't calm the storm,
so stop trying.
What you can do is calm yourself.
The storm will pass.
—**Timber Hawkeye**

59

— 14 —

LAY YOUR BURDEN DOWN

Come to me,
all you who are weary and burdened,
and I will give you rest.
Take my yoke upon you
and learn from me,
for I am gentle and humble in heart,
and you will find rest for your souls,
for my yoke is easy and my burden is light.
—**Matthew 11:28–30**

— 15 —

FINDING COURAGE TO FACE THE UNKNOWN

Tender and compassionate God, you are our steadfast
companion in the joyous times of our lives. When we rejoice,
you celebrate with us; when we are anxious and afraid, you
offer us a relationship where we can find courage to face
the unknown; when we weep with sadness, you are our
comforter. Help us believe that you receive us as we are,
and help us to entrust ourselves, with all our many struggles
and hopes, to your faithful and abiding care. Amen.
—**Unknown**

— 16 —

KNOW THYSELF

It's not that God, the environment, and other people cannot
help us to be happy or find satisfaction. It's just that our
happiness, satisfaction, and our understanding, even of God,
will be no deeper than our capacity to know ourselves inwardly,
to encounter the world from the deep comfort that comes
from being at home in one's own skin, from an intimate
familiarity with the ways of one's own mind and body.
—Jon Kabat-Zinn

— 17 —

EACH DAY IS A PRECIOUS GIFT; USE IT WELL

This is the beginning of a new day.
I can waste it or use it for good.
What I do today is important because I am
exchanging a day of my life for it.
When tomorrow comes, this day will be gone forever,
leaving in its place something I have traded for it.
I want it to be a gain, not a loss;
good, not evil;
success, not failure—
in order that I shall not regret the price I paid for it today.
—Jaya Khan

— 18 —

EVERYTHING WILL BE NEW AGAIN

As he sat by the river,
the eyes of his understanding began to be opened;
not that he saw any vision,
but he understood and learnt many things,
both spiritual matters and matters of faith and of scholarship,
and this with so great an enlightenment
that everything seemed new to him.

–Ignatius of Loyola

— 19 —

THE STORM WILL PASS

Never cut a tree down in the wintertime.
Never make a negative decision in the low time.
Never make your most important decisions
when you are in your worst moods.
Wait. Be patient.
The storm will pass.
The spring will come.

–Robert H. Schuller

— 20 —

CULTIVATE YOURSELF FULLY

To put the world right in order,
we must first put the nation in order;

To put the nation in order,
we must first put the family in order;

To put the family in order,
we must first cultivate our personal life;

We must first set our hearts right.

—Confucius

— 21 —

BE PRESENT TO THE LIFE YOU HAVE

In a true you-and-I relationship, we are present mindfully,
nonintrusively, the way we are present with things in
nature. We do not tell a birch tree it should be more like
an elm. We face it with no agenda, only an appreciation
that becomes participation: "I love looking at this birch,"
becomes "I am this birch," and then, "I and this birch are
opening to a mystery that transcends and holds us both."

—David Richo

— 22 —
TRUST YOUR HIGHEST POWER

May today there be peace within.
May you trust God that you are exactly
where you are meant to be.
May you not forget the infinite possibilities that are born of faith.
May you use those gifts that you have received, and
pass on the love that has been given to you.
May you be content knowing you are a child of God.
Let this presence settle into your bones, and allow your
soul the freedom to sing, dance, praise, and love.
It is there for each and every one of us.
Amen.

–Minnie Louise Haskins, *The Desert*, 1908

— 23 —
CREATE TRANQUILITY IN YOUR LIFE

The more tranquil a man becomes,
the greater is his success,
his influence, his power for good.
Calmness of mind is one of the beautiful jewels of wisdom.

–James Allen

– 24 –

BE FILLED WITH DEEP AND ABIDING PEACE

Deep peace I breathe into you,
O weariness, here:
O ache, here!
Deep peace, a soft white dove to you;
Deep peace, a quiet rain to you;
Deep peace, an ebbing wave to you!
Deep peace, red wind of the east from you;
Deep peace, grey wind of the west to you;
Deep peace, dark wind of the north from you;
Deep peace, blue wind of the south to you!
Deep peace, pure red of the flame to you;
Deep peace, pure white of the moon to you;
Deep peace, pure green of the grass to you;
Deep peace, pure brown of the earth to you;
Deep peace, pure grey of the dew to you,
Deep peace, pure blue of the sky to you!
Deep peace of the running wave to you,
Deep peace of the flowing air to you.

– Fiona Macleod, 1895

— 25 —

BASK IN THE WARMTH OF LOVE

The Lord bless you and keep you;
The Lord make his face shine upon you and be gracious to you;
The Lord turn his face toward you and give you peace.
–Numbers 6:24–26

— 26 —

JUST SURRENDER

God, who is more than we can ever comprehend,
help us to seek you
and you alone.
Help us to stand before all that we could do
and seek what you would do,
and do that.
Lift from us our need to achieve all that we can be
and instead,
surrender to what you can be in us.
Give us ways to refrain from the busyness
that will put us on edge and off center;
give us today your peace.
–Unknown

– 27 –

LEARN THE ART OF PATIENCE

Patience is waiting.
Not passively waiting.
That is laziness.
But to keep going
when the going is hard and slow—
that is patience.
–Leo Tolstoy

– 28 –

FACING THE FUTURE

Every journey begins
With but a small step.
And every day is a chance
For a new, small step
In the right direction.
Just follow your Heartsong.
–Mattie J. Stepanek

– 29 –

WE ARE ALL UNDER THE SAME SUN

The sun shines down,
and its image reflects a thousand
different pots filled with water.

The reflections are many,
but they are each reflecting the same sun.

Similarly, when we come to know who we truly are,
we will see ourselves in all people.

–Amma

— 30 —

INFINITE PEACE TO YOU

Deep peace of the running wave to you.
Deep peace of the flowing air to you.
Deep peace of the quiet earth to you.
Deep peace of the shining stars to you.
Deep peace of the infinite peace to you.

–Gaelic Blessing

— 31 —

Sometimes it seems when I'm talking to people about prayer
that one of the main points I have to keep making
over and over is there is no right way.
The important thing is to find your way...
You don't need any kind of noble or
highfalutin' or serious reason.
Any reason to begin a pattern of prayer is a good
reason because prayer is about everyday life.

–Roberta Bondi

PEACE, LOVE, AND SERENITY

"Everything you do can be done better
from a place of relaxation."
—*Stephen C. Paul*

"If the hurt comes, so will the happiness—be patient."
—*Rupi Kaur*

"Follow your bliss and the universe will open
doors where there were only walls."
—*Joseph Campbell*

"Let the peace of Christ rule in your hearts,
since as members of one body you were
called to peace. And be thankful."
—*Colossians 3:15*

"Cheerfulness keeps up a kind of daylight in the mind,
filling it with a steady and perpetual serenity."
—*Joseph Addison*

MINDFULNESS PRACTICE: SECURE AND GROUNDED

Quiet Observation Meditation

The quiet observation meditation is intended to bring you back to where you are and what you have already, all round you. I use it when I want to remind myself just how much life has given me—to appreciate it in a new and greater way.

Sit or stand in a comfortable position that you can easily maintain. Begin by taking a deep breath in, and, as you breathe out, slowly close your eyes. Take a few regular breaths and focus on your breathing, how your body moves with each intake, how your muscles soften each time you exhale. When you are ready, gently let go of that focus. Take a few moments to listen. What do you hear? Is there a faint buzzing from machinery? Can you hear the wind outside? Are people talking nearby? Be careful to observe your surroundings without judgment. When you are ready, open your eyes and slowly examine what you can see. Notice the details of every object around you. Acknowledge the existence of each and every thing that you can see and hear. When you have finished, let go of that observational focus and mindfully resume your day.

APRIL

SPRINGING BACK
FROM ANYTHING

"There are secrets opportunities hidden inside every failure."
   —*Sophia Amoruso*

"Many times, what we perceive as an error or failure is actually a gift. And eventually we find that lessons learned from that discouraging experience prove to be of great worth."
   —*Richelle E. Goodrich*

"In this life, we cannot do great things. We can only do small things with great love."
   —*Mother Teresa*

"Sometimes falling can be a new beginning too."
   —*Dhiman*

"Great works are performed not by strength but by perseverance."
   —*Samuel Johnson*

— 1 —

LIVE LIFE AS IF IT WERE A WORK OF ART

I would say to young people
a number of things, and I have only one minute.

I would say—let them remember
that there is a meaning beyond absurdity.

Let them be sure that every little deed counts,
that every word has power,

and that we do—everyone—our share
to redeem the world, in spite of all absurdities,
and all the frustrations, and all the disappointment.

And above all, remember that the meaning of life
is to live life as if it were a work of art.
—Rabbi Abraham Joshua Heschel

— 2 —

WE ARE ALL REBORN

It's okay
if you're burning
with anger
or sadness
or both
it is necessary

for you to collapse
so you can learn
how phoenixes are reborn
when they burn
and rise again
from the ashes of
their existence
–Noor Unnahar

— 3 —

Courage Takes Many Forms
Courage does not always roar.
Sometimes courage is the quiet voice
at the end of the day saying, "I will try again tomorrow."
–Mary Anne Radmacher

— 4 —

LIFE IS SHORT: BE KIND

Life is short and we have not too much time
for gladdening the hearts of those
who are traveling the dark way with us.
Oh, be swift to love! Make haste to be kind.
–Henri-Frederic Amiel, 1885

— 5 —

MAY ALL YOUR PRAYERS BE ANSWERED

May God give you...
For every storm, a rainbow
For every tear, a smile
For every case, a promise
And a blessing
In each trial
For every problem life sends,
A faithful friend to share
For every sigh a sweet song
And an answer
For each prayer.
—Irish prayer

— 6 —

DARE TO LOVE AND BE TRUE

I'm not trying to counsel any of you
to do anything really special
except to dare to think,
and to dare to go with the truth,
and to dare to really love completely.
—Buckminster Fuller

— 7 —

TOMORROW IS A NEW DAY

Finish each day and be done with it.
You have done what you could.
Some blunders and absurdities no doubt crept in;
forget them as soon as you can.
Tomorrow is a new day.
You shall begin it serenely
and with too high a spirit to be
encumbered with your old nonsense.
–Ralph Waldo Emerson

— 8 —

NEVER GIVE UP!

When things go wrong, as they sometimes will,
when the road you're trudging seems all uphill,
when the funds are low and the debts are high,
and you want to smile, but you have to sigh,
when care is pressing you down a bit,
rest, if you must–but don't you quit.

Life is queer with its twists and turns,
as every one of us sometimes learns,
and many a fellow turns about,
when he might have won had he stuck it out.
Don't give up, though the pace seems slow...
You might succeed with another blow.

Often the goal is nearer than it seems
to a faint and faltering man.
Often the struggler has given up,
when he might have captured the victor's cup,
and learned too late when the night slipped down,
How close he was to the golden crown.

Success is failure turned inside out,
the silver tint to the clouds of doubt–
And you can never tell how close you are.
It may appear when it seems afar;
So stick to the fight when you're hardest hit–
It's when things seem worst that you mustn't quit!

–Anonymous

– 9 –

MANTRAS ARE MEDITATIONS

Mantras...
are a mystical
sound vibration
encased
in a syllable.

–George Harrison

— 10 —

AWAKEN INTO YOUR STORY

May a good vision catch me
May a benevolent vision take hold of me, and move me
May a deep and full vision come over
me, and burst open around me
May a luminous vision inform me, enfold me.
May I awaken into the story that surrounds,
May I awaken into the beautiful story.
May the wondrous story find me;
May the wildness that makes beauty arise between two lovers
arise beautifully between my body and the body of this land,
between my flesh and the flesh of this earth,
here and now,
on this day,
May I taste something sacred.
–David Abram

— 11 —

WE ARE ALL MEANT TO SHINE

We are all meant to shine, as children do.
We were born to make manifest the
glory of God that is within us.
It is not just in some of us; it is in everyone.
And as we let our own light shine, we unconsciously
give other people permission to do the same.

As we are liberated from our own fear,
our presence automatically liberates others.
—Marianne Williamson

— 12 —

Live and Love and Forgive Yourself

I will write a letter to someone I haven't spoken with for a while.
I will send a message to someone I love dearly.
I will write a poem. I will make art.
I will play my guitar and sing.
I will volunteer myself to help loved ones and friends.
I will eat and drink healthy to show my body
my deep gratitude for its existence and the role
it plays in protecting my soul and spirit.

I will recite my mantras any time I feel
overwhelmed by thoughts that cause anxiety.
I will listen to someone who rarely has
the opportunity to be heard.
I will be aware of my breath and the rhythm of my heartbeat.

I will laugh and forgive myself when I forget
that I made these promises at the beginning of my day,
and at the end of my day I will celebrate and congratulate
myself for what I was able to accomplish.
—Julie Henderson

— 13 —
PATIENT ENDURANCE

No pain that we suffer,
no trial that we experience is wasted.
It ministers to our education,
to the development of such qualities as patience,
faith, fortitude, and humility.
All that we suffer and all that we endure,
especially when we endure it patiently,
builds up our characters, purifies our hearts,
expands our souls,
and makes us more tender and charitable,
more worthy to be called the children of God.
—Orson F. Whitney

— 14 —
SIMPLY DO THIS

Be still, and lay aside all thoughts of what you are
and what God is; all concepts you have learned
about the world; all images you hold about yourself.

Empty your mind of everything it thinks
is either true or false, or good or bad, of every thought it judges
worthy, and all the ideas of which it is ashamed.

Hold onto nothing.

Do not bring with you one thought the past has taught,
nor one belief you ever learned before from anything.

Forget this world, forget this course, and come
with wholly empty hands unto your God.
—**A Course in Miracles**

— 15 —

YOUR ACTIONS ARE YOUR ONLY TRUE BELONGINGS

I am of the nature to grow old.
There is no way to escape growing old.

I am of the nature to have ill-health.
There is no way to escape having ill-health.

I am of the nature to die.
There is no way to escape death.

All that is dear to me and all those I love
are of the nature to change.
There is no way to escape being separated from them.

My actions are my only true belongings.
I cannot escape the consequences of my actions.
My actions are the ground on which I stand.
—**Buddha**

— 16 —

WHAT IS STOPPING YOU?

The brick walls are there for a reason.
The brick walls are not there to keep us out.
The brick walls are there to give us a chance
to show how badly we want something.
Because the brick walls are there
to stop the people who don't want it badly enough.
They're there to stop the other people.
—Randy Pausch

— 17 —

JUST KEEP PUTTING ONE FOOT
IN FRONT OF THE OTHER

You never know what's around the corner.
It could be everything.
Or it could be nothing.
You keep putting one foot in front of the other,
and then one day you look back
and you've climbed a mountain.
—Tom Hiddleston

— 18 —

GOD UNROLLS THE CANVAS

My life is but a weaving
Between my Lord and me;
I cannot choose the colors
He weaveth steadily.
Oft' times He weaveth sorrow
And I in foolish pride
Forget He sees the upper
And I the underside.
Not till the loom is silent
And the shuttles cease to fly
Shall God unroll the canvas
And reveal the reason why.
The dark threads are as needful
In the weaver's skillful hand
As the threads of gold and silver
In the pattern He has planned.
He knows, He loves, He cares;
Nothing this truth can dim.
He gives the very best to those
Who leave the choice to Him.

—Florence May Alt

— 19 —

WHAT COMES AFTER DESPAIR

God does not send us despair in order to kill us;
He sends it in order to awaken us to new life.

–Hermann Hesse

— 20 —

FELLOWSHIP IS ALL

I do not think that the measure of a civilization
is how tall its buildings of concrete are,
but rather how well its people have learned to relate
to their environment and fellow man.

–Sun Bear

— 21 —

LOOK TO THE LIGHT

Believe more deeply.
Hold your face up to the light,
even though for the moment you do not see.

–Bill Wilson, Alcoholics Anonymous

– 22 –

QUIET THE MIND

God, please put a guard at my mouth,
love in my heart
and calm in my mind.

Amen

–Julia Lapianka

– 23 –

MAKE AWARENESS YOUR HOME

I have no parents:
I make the heaven and earth my parents.

I have no home:
I make awareness my home.

I have no life and death:
I make the tides of breathing my life and death.

I have no divine powers:
I make honesty my divine power.

I have no means:
I make understanding my means.

I have no secrets:
I make character my secret.

I have no body:
I make endurance my body.

I have no eyes:
I make the flash of lightning my eyes.

I have no ears:
I make sensibility my ears.

I have no limbs:
I make promptness my limbs.

I have no strategy:
I make "unshadowed by thought" my strategy.

I have no design:
I make "seizing opportunity by the forelock" my design.

I have no miracles:
I make right action my miracle.

I have no principles:
I make adaptability to all circumstances my principle.

I have no tactics:
I make emptiness and fullness my tactics.

I have no talent:
I make ready with my talent.

I have no friends:
I make my mind my friend.

I have no enemy:
I make carelessness my enemy.

I have no armor:
I make benevolence and righteousness my armor.

I have no castle:
I make my immovable mind my castle.

I *have no sword:*
I make absence of self my sword.
–Samuari Song, fourteenth century

– 24 –

LEARN AND GROW

Failures are part of life.
If you don't fail,
you don't learn.
If you don't learn,
you'll never change.
–Walter Hiram Harmon

– 25 –

THE FIRST HABIT OF HIGHLY EFFECTIVE HUMANS

Most of the important things in the world
have been accomplished by people
who have kept on trying
when there seemed to be no hope at all.
–Dale Carnegie

— 26 —

HOW TO LIVE A MAGICAL LIFE

It is impossible to live without failing at something,
unless you live so cautiously
that you might as well not have lived at all.
In which case, you fail by default.
–J.K. Rowling

— 27 —

PEACE IN THE HOME, PEACE IN THE HEART

If there is to be peace in the world,
There must be peace in the nations.

If there is to be peace in the nations,
There must be peace in the cities.

If there is to be peace in the cities,
There must be peace between neighbors.

If there is to be peace between neighbors,
There must be peace in the home.

If there is to be peace in the home,
There must be peace in the heart.

–Lao Tse

— 28 —

LOOK TO THE SUN

After every storm, the sun will smile;
for every problem, there is a solution,
and the soul's indefeasible duty is to be of good cheer.
—William R. Alger

— 29 —

ON THIS LONG, ROUGH ROAD

Promise me,
promise me this day,
promise me now,
while the sun is overhead
exactly at the zenith,
promise me:

Even as they
strike you down
with a mountain of hatred and violence;
even as they step on you and crush you
like a worm,
even as they dismember and disembowel you,
remember, brother,
remember:
man is not our enemy.

The only thing worthy of you is compassion—
invincible, limitless, unconditional.

89

Hatred will never let you face
the beast in man.

One day, when you face this beast alone,
with your courage intact, your eyes kind,
untroubled
(even as no one sees them),
out of your smile
will bloom a flower.

And those who love you
will behold you
across ten thousand worlds of birth and dying.

Alone again,
I will go on with bent head,
knowing that love has become eternal.
On the long, rough road,
the sun and the moon
will continue to shine.

– Thích Nhất Hạnh

— 30 —

FOUR VERY IMPORTANT SENTENCES IN LIFE

Please forgive me.
I forgive you.
Thank you.
I love you.

—Ira Byock

RULES FOR RESILIENCE

"The key of persistence opens all doors closed by resistance."
—*John Di Lemme*

"Come what may, all bad fortune is to be conquered by endurance."
—*Virgil*

"But as for you, be strong and do not give up, for your work will be rewarded."
—*2 Chronicles 15:7*

"Do not fear mistakes. You will know failure. Continue to reach out."
—*Benjamin Franklin*

"The man who moves a mountain begins by carrying away small stones."
—*Confucius*

PRAYERFUL PRACTICE: THE HEALING POWER OF TIME IN NATURE

The purpose of a nature-focused meditative walk is to remind you of all the natural beauty that exists around you every day. I like to do it whenever I've spent much of the day (or the week) inside, especially if I've been focused primarily on difficult tasks or complaints.

Begin by standing still outside. Take a deep breath in and let it out, then take your first step, walking and breathing normally, not too fast and not too slow. As you walk, take notice of your surroundings. Look for pockets of nature—is grass peeking through the cracks in the sidewalk? Are there trees and bushes anywhere? How about flowers? Look for green plants, brown earth, blue or gray sky. Is it cold or warm? Bright or cloudy? Continue your walk and observe your surroundings without judging them: let them be what they are.

MAY

BLOOMING UNDER

PRESSURE

"It always seems impossible until it is done."
   —*Nelson Mandela*

"If you hear the dogs, keep on going. If you hear gunfire, keep on going. If you hear shouts and footsteps, keep on going."
   —*Harriet Tubman*

"Doubt kills more dreams than failure ever will."
   —*Suzy Kassem*

"Nothing in nature blooms all year. Be patient with yourself."
   —*Unknown*

"And now that you don't have to be perfect, you can be good."
   —*John Steinbeck*

— 1 —

OUR SPIRITS ARE BEING RENEWED EVERY DAY

We are pressed on every side by troubles,
but we are not crushed and broken.
We are perplexed, but we don't give up and quit.
That is why we never give up.
Though our bodies are dying,
our spirits are being renewed every day.
For our present troubles are quite small
and won't last very long.
Yet they produce for us an immeasurably
great glory that will last forever!
–2 Corinthians 4:8-18

— 2 —

THE WRITER'S PRAYER

Awaken to a new dawn,
I stretch to Infinity 'n reach Beyond the Stars,
In an instant I return,
filling every tissue, sinew, with Joy,
I feed the nectar of life, into each molecule and cell,
The mind and body embrace Divine love
Through the eye of time I see eternity,
Life in life shine bright,

Shine the torch of majestic light,
Find the path to my universal frame,
So I may bask in the wisdom of pure potential,
Guide my hand to write your words.
—**Michael Levy**

— 3 —

FOR THEY SHALL BE CALLED THE CHILDREN OF GOD

Blessed are the poor in spirit:
for theirs is the kingdom of heaven.
Blessed are they that mourn:
for they shall be comforted.
Blessed are the meek:
for they shall inherit the earth.
Blessed are they which do hunger and thirst after righteousness:
for they shall be filled.
Blessed are the merciful:
for they shall obtain mercy.
Blessed are the pure in heart:
for they shall see God.
Blessed are the peacemakers:
for they shall be called the children of God.
Blessed are they which are persecuted for righteousness' sake:
for theirs is the kingdom of heaven.
—**Matthew 5:3–10**

— 4 —

WE ARE NURTURED BY THE SAME EARTH

Out beyond ideas of wrongdoing and rightdoing,
there is a field. I'll meet you there.
When the soul lies down in that grass,
the world is too full to talk about.
Ideas, language, even the phrase "each
other" doesn't make any sense.
—Rumi, 13th century Persian poet

— 5 —

SING TO ME

Come sister, come sing to me.
We are both enlivened by the same spirit,
We are both nurtured by the same earth.

I feel your roots beneath the earth, beneath me
I am in awe of your majesty

Your limbs stretch to the heavens
Letting in just enough light for me to find my own way.
You sing softly to me in the breeze

I am at peace here.
I am home here.
I am safe here.
I am free to think my thoughts and hear your whispers,

"Stay free for me, come sing with me.
We are both enlivened by the same spirit,
We are both nurtured by the same earth.
Come sister, come sing with me."
—Adrienne O'Hare

— 6 —

YOU ARE SHELTERED FROM THE STORM

All shall
be well,
and all shall
be well,
and all manner
of thing
shall be well.
—Julian of Norwich, 14th century

— 7 —

THE HEART IS WIDE

The world stands out on either side
No wider than the heart is wide;
Above the world is stretched the sky,
No higher than the soul is high.
The heart can push the sea and land

Farther away on either hand;
The soul can split the sky in two,
And let the face of God shine through.
But East and West will pinch the heart
That cannot keep them pushed apart;
And he whose soul is flat—the sky
Will cave in on him by and by.
— **Edna St. Vincent Millay**

— 8 —

TELL GOD WHAT YOU NEED

Don't worry about anything,
instead pray about everything.
Tell God what you need,
and thank him for all he has done.

If you do this, you will experience God's peace,
which is far more wonderful
than the human mind can understand.
His peace will guard your hearts and minds
as you live in Christ Jesus.
—**Philippians 4:4-7**

— 9 —

PAY ATTENTION SO YOU DON'T MISS THE MIRACLES

By some incredible miracle,
the vast ocean of time has borne me up
to its crest for this miniscule moment.
I look around, revel in all that I see,
feel the spray in my face,
elated by the majesty,
the enormity of creation,
grateful beyond belief to be alive.
—Hal French

— 10 —

YOU CAN DO ANYTHING

Start by doing what's necessary;
then do what's possible;
and suddenly
you are doing the impossible.
—Saint Francis of Assisi

— 11 —

JUST BELIEVE

Faith is the first factor
in a life devoted to service.

Without it, nothing is possible.
With it, nothing is impossible.
–Mary McLeod Bethune

— 12 —

LIVE THE QUESTIONS NOW

Have patience with everything unresolved in your heart
and try to love the questions themselves...
Don't search for the answers,
which could not be given to you now,
because you would not be able to live them.
And the point is, to live everything.
Live the questions now.
Perhaps then, someday far in the future,
you will gradually, without even noticing it,
live your way into the answer.
–Rainer Maria Rilke

— 13 —

THE DOOR WILL OPEN

Keep on asking,
and you will receive
what you ask for.
Keep on seeking,
and you will find.

Keep on knocking,
and the door
will be opened to you.
—**Matthew 7:7**

— 14 —

CHERISH THE SIMPLE THINGS

Each day is a blessing
of epic proportions.
I give thanks for
what might seem meager comforts:
real cream in my coffee,
a day without a bill in the mail...
—**Ruth Williams**

— 15 —

MOVING HEAVEN AND EARTH

Nothing is impossible in this world.
Firm determination, it is said,
can move heaven and earth.
Things appear far beyond one's power
because one cannot set his heart
on any arduous project due to want of strong will.
—**Yamamoto Tsunetomo**

— 16 —

BE BRAVE, FOR THERE IS MUCH TO DARE

I would be true, for there are those who trust me;
I would be pure, for there are those who care;
I would be strong, for there is much to suffer;
I would be brave, for there is much to dare;
I would be brave, for there is much to dare.

I would be friend of all–the foe, the friendless;
I would be giving, and forget the gift;
I would be humble, for I know my weakness;
I would look up, and laugh, and love and lift.
I would look up, and laugh, and love and lift.
–Howard Arnold Walter, 1906

— 17 —

REMEMBER

When everything seems to be going against you,
remember that the airplane takes off
against the wind, not with it.
–Henry Ford

— 18 —

HARBOR IN GOOD

I celebrate myself, and sing myself,
And what I assume you shall assume,
For every atom belonging to me as good belongs to you.

I loafe and invite my soul,
I lean and loafe at my ease observing a spear of summer grass.

My tongue, every atom of my blood,
form'd from this soil, this air,
Born here of parents born here from parents
the same, and their parents the same,
I, now thirty-seven years old in perfect health begin,
Hoping to cease not till death.

Creeds and schools in abeyance,
Retiring back a while sufficed at what
they are, but never forgotten,
I harbor for good or bad, I permit to speak at every hazard,
Nature without check with original energy.
—Walt Whitman, *Song of Myself*

— 19 —

SEVEN STEPS TO EFFECTIVE PRAYER

1.

I release all of my past, negatives,
fears, human relationships, self-image, future,
and human desires to the Light.

2.

I am a Light Being.

3.

I radiate the Light from my Light Center
throughout my being.

4.

I radiate the Light
from my Light Center to everyone.

5.

I radiate the Light
from my Light Center to everything.

6.

I am in a bubble of Light
and only Light can come to me
and only Light can be here.

7.

Thank you, God, for everyone, for everything and for me.

—Jim Goure

— 20 —

BE UNSTOPPABLE

Obstacles don't have to stop you.
If you run into a wall,
don't turn around and give up.

Figure out how to climb it,
go through it,
or work around it.
–Michael Jordan

— 21 —

KEEP HOLDING ON

Hold on to what is good
even if it is
a handful of earth.
Hold on to what you believe
even if it is
a tree which stands by itself.
Hold on to what you must do
even if it is
a long way from here.
Hold on to life even when
it is easier letting go.
Hold on to my hand even when
I have gone away from you.
–Nancy Wood

— 22 —

FAITH LIKE A MUSTARD SEED

He said to them, 'Because of your little faith.
For truly, I say to you, if you have faith
like a grain of mustard seed,
you will say to this mountain,
"Move from here to there,"
and it will move,
and nothing will be impossible for you.
—Matthew 17:20

— 23 —

INFINITE GOODNESS

I had a few days ago an insight which consoled me very much.
It was during my thanksgiving, when I make
a few reflections upon the goodness of God, and
how should one not think of this at such a time, of that
infinite goodness, uncreated goodness, the source of all goodness...

I saw written as in letters of gold this word, "Goodness"
which I repeated for a long time with indescribable sweetness.
I beheld it, I say, written upon all creatures,
animate and inanimate,
rational or not, all bore this name goodness...

I understood then that all these creatures have of goodness and
all the services and assistance that we receive from each of them
is a benefit which we owe to the goodness of God

who has communicated to them something
of his infinite goodness
so that we may meet it in everything and everywhere.
–St. Thérèse Couderc, 1865

— 24 —

BE A BETTER VERSION OF YOU

Always dream and shoot higher
than you know you can do.
Don't bother just to be better
than your contemporaries or predecessors.
Try to be better than yourself.
–**William Faulkner**

— 25 —

BLUE TRUE DREAM OF SKY

I thank You God for this amazing
day: for the leaping greenly spirits of trees
and a blue true dream of sky; and for everything
which is natural which is infinite which is yes

(I who have died am alive again today,
and this is the sun's birthday; this is the birth
day of life and of love and wings: and of the gay
great happening illimitably earth)

how should tasting touching hearing seeing
breathing any–lifted from the no
of all nothing–human merely being
doubt unimaginable You?
(now the ears of my ears awake and
now the eyes of my eyes are opened)
—e. e. cummings

— 26 —

IN THE LIGHT OF EACH DAY

In the joy of your heart,
Your light remains.

In the gift of your caring,
Your light remains

Where you reached out to help,
Your light remains.

Where you sat in silent peace,
Your light remains.

In the place where you worked,
Your light remains

In the stillness of the starry night,
Your light remains

In the light of each day fully embraced,
Your light remains.

Like the touch of an Angel,
Your light remains.

When you live as a light,
Your heart is joined in the Infinite Light of Love.
And that about you which is eternal...*remains.*
–Reverend Jacquie Riker

— 27 —

TRUE GRACE

Carry out a random act of kindness,
with no expectation of reward,
safe in the knowledge
that one day someone
might do the same for you.
–Princess Diana

— 28 —

THERE IS NO JOY IN THINGS THAT DON'T EXIST

In humility is the greatest freedom.
As long as you have to defend the imaginary self
that you think is important, you lose your peace of heart.
As soon as you compare that shadow
with the shadows of other people, you lose all joy,

because you have begun to trade in unrealities
and there is no joy in things that do not exist.
–Thomas Merton

– 29 –

HOW TO PRAY

Jesus taught that effective prayer must be:
Unselfish–not alone for oneself.
Believing–according to faith.
Sincere–honest of heart.
Intelligent–according to light.
Trustful–in submission to the Father's all-wise will.
–Byron Belitsos

– 30 –

BECOME A MIGHTY EXPRESSION OF LOVE

Let my heart be the vessel of God's Love.
Let my thoughts be the blossom of God's Love.
Let my words be the expression of God's Love.
Let my actions be the fulfillment of God's Love.
–David Ridge

— 31 —

FORGIVENESS IS THE KEY TO EVERYTHING

Nothing that is worth doing can be achieved in our lifetime;
therefore, we must be saved by hope.

Nothing which is true or beautiful or good makes
complete sense in any immediate context of history;
therefore, we must be saved by faith.

Nothing we do, however virtuous, could be accomplished alone;
therefore, we must be saved by love.

No virtuous act is quite as virtuous from the standpoint
of our friend or foe as it is from our own standpoint;
therefore, we must be saved by the final
form of love, which is forgiveness.
—**Reinhold Niebuhr**

"The limits of the possible can only be defined
by going beyond them into the impossible."
—*Arthur C. Clarke*

"If you were born with the weakness to fall,
you were born with the strength to rise."
—*Rupi Kaur, Milk and Honey*

"The greatest glory in living lies not in never
falling, but in rising every time we fall."
—*Oliver Goldsmith, 1762*

"Tough times never last, but tough people do."
—*Robert Schuller*

"If you fall behind, run faster. Never give up, never
surrender, and rise up against the odds."
—*Jesse Jackson*

"True progress quietly and persistently
moves along without notice."
—*St. Francis of Assisi*

TAKE TIME FOR TRANQUILITY: SELF-CARE PRACTICE

If you had a rough day at work, your inner critic was overactive, or you're just feeling a little down, try this lovingkindness meditation. It can be difficult to cultivate self-love, but it is one of the most important things you can do for yourself. The very peacefulness you create with this ritual can also be sent to another with your intention. Begin by sitting quietly, taking relaxed, slow, deep breaths and wishing yourself happiness. After sitting quietly, begin to speak this mantra aloud:

May I be happy.
May I be well.
May I be safe.
May I be peaceful.
May I be at ease.
May I be content.

Continue this practice until you feel "full" of self-love and compassion. When you are ready to move to the next phase, begin to think of another person to whom you would like to give happiness and unconditional love. Send the love through your meditation and by saying these words:

May you be happy.
May you be well.
May you be safe.
May you be peaceful.
May you be filled with contentment

JUNE

BLESSINGS FOR WHEN YOU'RE STRESSING

"Why worry? If you've done the very best you can, worrying won't make it any better."
   —*Walt Disney*

"What's comin' will come, and we'll meet it when it does."
   —*Hagrid, Harry Potter*

"And not only that, but we also glory in tribulations, knowing that tribulation produces perseverance; and perseverance, character; and character, hope."
   —*Romans 5:3–4*

"We are formed by environment and grace, by politics and prayer, by church and conscience. All God's creatures conspire to teach us as well. We stumble. We stutter. We rise. We are lifted."
   —*Saint Anthony of Padua*

"The greatest weapon against stress is our ability to choose one thought over another."
   —*Anonymous*

117

— 1 —

THERE IS BEAUTY IN THE STRUGGLE

Success is not measured by what you accomplish
but by the opposition you have encountered
and the courage with which
you have maintained the struggle
against overwhelming odds.
—Orison Swett Marden

— 2 —

SWEET MERCY

My soul is weary.
Worry, fear, and doubt
Surround me,
On every side.

Yet your sweet mercy
Cannot be held back
From those that cry out to you.
Hear my cry.

Let me trust in your mercy.
Show me how. Free me.
Free me from anxiety and stress

That I may find rest
In your loving arms.
Amen.
–Anonymous

— 3 —

WORRY DOESN'T HELP; IT DOES THE OPPOSITE

Look at the birds of the air;
they do not sow or reap or store away in barns,
and yet your heavenly Father feeds them.
Are you not much more valuable than they?
Can any one of you by worrying add a single hour to your life?
–Matthew 6:26–27

— 4 —

GRATEFUL FOR MY CHANCE TO GROW

Sky above me Earth below me
flying swirling through the all
seeds of love are growing in me
all of nature blooms along
grace and joy I am unfolding
grateful for my chance to grow
–Lizabeth Gottsegen

119

— 5 —

PRAYER FOR HEALING

I realize that the body is not separate from the mind
As I let go my old attitude toward my body
I appreciate the influence of the spirit and soul
And I embrace my body and my entire self

My body is a reflection of my thoughts
As I give myself positive affirmations
I release my negative emotions and thoughts
And I let my body be healed as well as my mind

I am willing to get better and heal
I am lifted above the areas of my pain
I am rising beyond my suffering
I am releasing my desperation

I understand and accept my insecurities
I feel compassion toward my pains
I surrender my terror for it is not real
From my body, heart, and soul
I do my best to fill myself with love
I expect a miracle with relaxed anticipation

I am my own best doctor and advisor
I am a catalyst for healing
I am a producer of health
I am a creator of happiness

Thank you for my healing body

Thank you for my gentle soul
Thank you for my strong spirit
Thank you for the chance to heal

I am willing to be enlightened as
I am blessed with this wisdom
I deserve to be healthy and happy and
I claim my perfect health again

I am ONE and I am LOVING.
I am HERE and I am NOW.
I am HEALED and I am WHOLE.
Thank YOU. Let it Be! And SO IT IS!
—Darina Stoyanova

— 6 —

SWEET SEASONS OF LIFE

O sweet spontaneous
earth how often have
the
doting

            fingers of
prurient philosophies pinched
and
poked

thee
, has the naughty thumb

of science prodded
thy

        beauty   .how
        often have religions taken
        thee upon their scraggy
        knees squeezing and
buffeting thee that thou mightest conceive
gods

        (but

true

to the incomparable
couch of death thy
rhythmic
lover

        thou answerest
them only with

        spring)
        –e. e. cummings

– 7 –

BE FILLED WITH EASE TODAY

May I be filled with loving kindness.
May I be well.
May I be peaceful and at ease.
May I be happy.
–Ancient Buddhist Chant

– 8 –

DEEP RELIEF

Deep relief, that's what I know I'm needing,
Sweet release from all I've locked inside.
A full reprieve from all my fears and worry.
I long to feel the part where love expands my heart
And I no longer need a place to hide.

Move in slow, so I can hear your breathing.
Take my hand so I can know your touch.
Just to be inside this silent stillness–
My heart has no defense to offer up against
The endless ache of opening this much.

I'm on fire, you see it in my face,
I'm alive with the splendor and the grace.
You are welcome to join me in this space
And journey on the quest to love our very best
And live within this intimate embrace.

–Ellen Robinson

– 9 –

SHELTER OF THE NIGHT

For each new morning with its light,
For rest and shelter of the night,
For health and food,

For love and friends,
For everything Thy goodness sends.
–Ralph Waldo Emerson

— 10 —

PEACE IN EVERY STEP

God be between you and harm in
all the empty places you walk.
–Egyptian Blessing, 1729

— 11 —

ARMS CLASPED AROUND THE WORLD

I like how God feels around
everyone in the world.
God, I am very happy that
I live on you.
Your arms clasp around the world.
I like you and your friends.
Every time I open my eyes
I see the gleaming sun.
I like the animals–the deer,
and us creatures of the world,
the mammals.
I love my dear friends.
–Danu Baxter

— 12 —

HATE WON'T WIN

Hate won't win
Hate won't win
Hate won't win
Though you try to destroy me
I still forgive you
Though you try to undo me
The mercy of God surrounds you
Hate won't win
Lord have mercy on your soul
God have mercy on us all
Hate won't win
–Benjamin Mertz

— 13 —

THE JOY IN A HEART THAT BEATS

Peace.
Peace, She says to me.
Peace to your soul.
I am the beauty in the leaf.
I am the echo in a baby's laugh.
I am your Mother.
I am the joy in the heart that beats.
I am the free woman.

I am the one who breaks the shackles of oppression.
You are my hands and feet.
—**Gaian Prayer**

— 14 —

WORRYING WILL NOT SOLVE YOUR PROBLEM

When you begin to worry,
go find something to do.
Get busy being a blessing to someone;
do something fruitful...
Above all else,
remember that worrying is totally useless.
Worrying will not solve your problem.
—**Joyce Meyer**

— 15 —

SEND YOUR WORRIES DOWNSTREAM

A thousand ages in Thy sight
Are like an evening gone;
Short as the watch that ends the night
Before the rising sun.

The busy tribes of flesh and blood,
With all their cares and fears,
Are carried downward by the flood,
And lost in following years.
—Isaac Waats, 1710

— 16 —

LIVING, BREATHING, MOVING

Praise, thanksgiving, celebration
and congratulations to God,

The One,
Living, Breathing, Moving,
Active Holy Energy,
Living Spirit,
Creator of the Universe,
of the Oversoul
and of me
and of thee.
—Luz Antigua

— 17 —

FILL THE DAY WITH LOVE

Start the Day with Love;
Spend the Day with Love;

Fill the Day with Love;
End the Day with Love;
This is the way to God.
—Sri Sathya Sai Baba

— 18 —

LAUGHING MAKES EVERYTHING BETTER

Since things neither exist nor don't exist,
are neither real nor unreal,
are utterly beyond adopting and rejecting—
one might as well burst out laughing.
—Longchenpa Rabjampa, 1388

— 19 —

THE SUN WILL SOMETIMES MELT A FIELD OF SORRY

Sometimes things don't go, after all,
from bad to worse. Some years, muscadel
faces down frost; green thrives; the crops don't fail.
Sometimes a man aims high, and all goes well.

A people sometimes will step back from war,
elect an honest man, decide they care
enough, that they can't leave some stranger poor.
Some men become what they were born for.

Sometimes our best efforts do not go
amiss; sometimes we do as we meant to.
The sun will sometimes melt a field of sorrow
that seemed hard frozen; may it happen for you.
–Sheenagh Pugh

– 20 –

GUIDED, GUARDED, AND PROTECTED

The light of God surrounds us;
The love of God enfolds us;
The power of God protects us;
The presence of God watches over us.
Wherever we are, God is.
And all is well.
–Unity Song

– 21 –

MAY YOUR DAYS BE HAPPY IN NUMBER AS FLAKES OF SNOW

The winter will lose its cold,
as the snow will be without whiteness,
The night without darkness,
the heavens without stars,
the day without light,
The flower will lose its beauty,

all fountains their water,
the sea its fish,
the tree its birds,
the forest its beasts,
the earth its harvest–
All these things will pass before
anyone breaks the bonds of our love,
And before I cease caring for you in my heart.
May your days be happy in number as flakes of snow,
May your nights be peaceful,
and may you be without troubles.
—Matthew of Revaulx, 1270

— 22 —

THERE IS A BALM IN GILEAD

There is a balm in Gilead
To make the wounded whole;
There is a balm in Gilead
To heal the sin-sick soul.

Sometimes I feel discouraged,
And think my work's in vain,
But then the Holy Spirit
Revives my soul again.

There is a balm in Gilead
To make the wounded whole;

There is a balm in Gilead
To heal the sin-sick soul.

If you can't preach like Peter,
If you can't pray like Paul,
Just tell the love of Jesus
And say He died for all.

There is a balm in Gilead
To make the wounded whole;
There is a balm in Gilead
To heal the sin-sick soul.
–African American Spiritual

— 23 —

OPEN THE WINDOW TO LOVE

There is some kiss we want
with our whole lives,
the touch of Spirit on the body.
Seawater begs the pearl
to break its shell.
And the lily, how passionately
it needs some wild Darling!
At night, I open the window
and ask the moon to come
and press its face into mine.
Breathe into me.
Close the language-door,

131

and open the love-window.
The moon won't use the door,
only the window.
–Rumi, 13th century Persian poet

— 24 —

AN OFFERING FOR YOUR DELIGHT

To our Gods of old, we bless the ground
that you tread in search of our freedom!
We bless your presence in our lives and in our hearts!
Take of this offering to your delight,
and be filled with our prayers of thanksgiving!
May our lives remain as full as our hearts on this day!
–Yoruban Chant

— 25 —

NO WORRIES

The Bible says not to worry,
so I don't.
I just get up in the morning
and ask God for help to get through the day.
If tomorrow shows up,
then I'll take the same shot tomorrow.
–Paul Henderson

— 26 —

THE GIFT OF CRISIS

Emotional discomfort,
when accepted,
rises, crests, and falls
in a series of waves.
Each wave
washes parts of us away
and deposits treasures
we never imagined.
–Martha Beck

— 27 —

DROP LOVE BOMBS EVERYWHERE

Poems
Hugs
Music
Photography
Movies
Kind words
Smiles

Meditation and prayer
Dance
Social activism
Websites
Blogs
Random acts of kindness
—The Spiritual Revolutionaries

— 28 —

MAKE MISTAKES AND GROW

Our children who live on earth,
Holy are each and every one of you.
May good dreams come,
Your way be found,
And heaven and earth rejoice with you.

May you be given
All you need for life
And may you accept our mistakes
As you allow yourself
To make mistakes and grow.

Lead us with imagination
And true integrity,
For yours are the minds, the hearts, and the souls
To heal the world
Now and forever.
—Roberto Leffler

— 29 —

PRAY LOUD

Wage peace with your listening: hearing sirens, pray loud.
Remember your tools: flower seeds, clothes pins, clean rivers.
Make soup.
Play music, memorize the words for thank you in three languages.
Learn to knit, and make a hat.
Think of chaos as dancing raspberries,
imagine grief
as the outbreath of beauty
or the gesture of fish.
Swim for the other side.
Wage peace.
Never has the world seemed so fresh and precious:
Have a cup of tea and rejoice.
Act as if armistice has already arrived.
Celebrate today.

—Judyth Hill

— 30 —

SIT IN STILLNESS

You do not need to leave your room.

Remain sitting at your table and listen.

Do not even listen. Simply wait.

Do not even wait. Be quiet, still and solitary.

The world will freely offer itself to you to be unmasked.

It has no choice. It will roll in ecstasy at your feet.

—Franz Kafka, 1918

WORRY BEADS, ROSARIES, AND OTHER WAYS TO PRAY

"Worrying means you suffer twice."
—*Newt Scamander, Fantastic Beasts and Where to Find Them*

"Sometimes we have to stop being scared and just go for it. Either it'll work or it won't. That is life."
—*Alex Elle*

"Life is too short to worry about anything. You had better enjoy it because the next day promises nothing."
—*Eric Davis*

"Adopting the right attitude can convert a negative stress into a positive one."
—*Hans Selye*

"Stress and worry, they solve nothing. What they do is block creativity. You are not even able to think about the solutions. Every problem has a solution."

—*Susan L. Taylor*

"I believe God is managing affairs and that he doesn't need any advice from me. With God in charge, I believe everything will work out for the best in the end. So, what is there to worry about?"

—*Henry Ford*

CHOP WOOD, CARRY WATER, SWEEP FLOORS: FINDING YOUR ZEN

After I graduated from college, I had one of those experiences we all must endure in our twenties: a bad breakup. I was somewhat of a zombie, but my best friend, who was studying Zen Buddhism, was of a more practical bent. She placed a broom in my hand and suggested I "stop thinking about anything but doing the best possible job sweeping the floor." I took her advice and even swept the sidewalks once I was done with the small cottage we lived in. Sweeping did bring about a stillness inside me, which was a relief after all the turmoil. I was still hurting, but the simplicity of the chores engendered quietude. I have a few brooms, and one is always right outside the back door and ready for the simple ritual of sweeping. I even developed a mantra to go with my sweeping meditation:

No storm outside, no storm within,
With every stroke and every step,
I feel more peace and quiet inside me.
Blessings to all. Blessed be me.

I have had times where I needed to sweep every floor and even the lawn outside, but it is immensely meditative and I encourage you also to find your Zen.

139

STAYING CALM WHEN ANXIETY STRIKES

"The world only exists in your eyes. You can make it as big or as small as you want."
  —*F. Scott Fitzgerald*

"Bravery is being terrified and doing it anyway."
  —*Laurell K. Hamilton*

"Everything is going to be okay in the end. If it's not okay, it's not the end."
  —*John Lennon*

"Do not be anxious about anything, but in everything, by prayer and petition, with thanksgiving, present your requests to God. And the peace of God, which transcends all understanding, will guard your hearts and your minds in Christ Jesus."
  —*Philippians 4:6–7*

"Humble yourselves, therefore, under the mighty hand of God so that at the proper time he may exalt you, casting all your anxieties on him, because he cares for you."
  —*1 Peter 5:6–7*

141

"Do not let your difficulties fill you with anxiety; after all, it is only in the darkest nights that stars shine more brightly."
  —*Ali Talib*

— 1 —

NO AMOUNT OF ANXIETY CAN CHANGE YOUR FUTURE

When thinking about life,
remember this:
no amount of guilt
can change the past
and no amount of anxiety
can change the future.

–Unknown

— 2 —

KEEP TO THE SUNNY SIDE OF LIFE

There's a dark and a troubled side of life;
There's a bright and a sunny side, too;
Tho' we meet with the darkness and strife,
The sunny side we also may view.

Keep on the sunny side, always on the sunny side,
Keep on the sunny side of life;
It will help us every day, it will brighten all the way,
If we keep on the sunny side of life.

Tho' the storm in its fury break today,
Crushing hopes that we cherished so dear,
Storm and cloud will in time pass away,
The sun again will shine bright and clear.

Keep on the sunny side, always on the sunny side,
Keep on the sunny side of life;
It will help us every day, it will brighten all the way,
If we keep on the sunny side of life.

Let us greet with a song of hope each day,
Tho' the moments be cloudy or fair;
Let us trust in our Savior always,
Who keepeth everyone in His care.

Keep on the sunny side, always on the sunny side,
Keep on the sunny side of life;
It will help us every day, it will brighten all the way,
If we keep on the sunny side of life.
—**Ada Blenkhorn, 1899**

— 3 —

MOVE AND GROOVE

When you pray,
move your feet.
—**African Proverb**

— 4 —

EVERY DAY IS SACRED

With visible breath I am walking.
A voice I am sending as I walk.
In a sacred manner I am walking.
With visible tracks I am walking.
In a sacred manner I walk.

—Native American Chant

— 5 —

TODAY IS THE RIGHT DAY TO LIVE

He said, "There are only two days in the year
that nothing can be done.
One is called *yesterday*
and the other is called *tomorrow*,
so today is the right day to love, believe, do and mostly live."

—Dalai Lama

— 6 —

SIMPLE GIFTS

'Tis the gift to be simple, 'tis the gift to be free,
'Tis the gift to come down where we ought to be,
And when we find ourselves in the place just right,
'Twill be in the valley of love and delight.
When true simplicity is gain'd,

To bow and to bend we shan't be asham'd,
To turn, turn will be our delight,
Till by turning, turning we come 'round right.
–Shaker Elder Joseph Brackett, 1848

– 7 –

FILLING YOUR CUP

The grief you cry out from
draws you toward union.

Your pure sadness
that wants help
is the secret cup.

Listen to the moan of a dog for its master.
That whining is the connection.

There are love dogs
no one knows the names of.

Give your life
to be one of them.
–Rumi, 13th century Persian poet

– 8 –

YOU ARE SUPPORTED

The will of God will never take you,
Where the grace of God cannot keep you.
Where the arms of God cannot support you,
Where the riches of God cannot supply your needs,
Where the power of God cannot endow you.

The will of God will never take you,
Where the spirit of God cannot work through you,
Where the wisdom of God cannot teach you,
Where the army of God cannot protect you,
Where the hands of God cannot mold you.

The will of God will never take you,
Where the love of God cannot enfold you,
Where the mercies of God cannot sustain you,
Where the peace of God cannot calm your fears,
Where the authority of God cannot overrule for you.

The will of God will never take you,
Where the comfort of God cannot dry your tears,
Where the Word of God cannot feed you,
Where the miracles of God cannot be done for you,
Where the omnipresence of God cannot find you.

–Unknown

– 9 –

HOLY BIRDS AT THE KITCHEN WINDOW

here is joy
in all:
in the hair I brush each morning,
in the Cannon towel, newly washed,
that I rub my body with each morning,
in the chapel of eggs I cook
each morning,
in the outcry from the kettle
that heats my coffee
each morning,
in the spoon and the chair
that cry "hello there, Anne,"
each morning,
in the godhead of the table
that I set my silver, plate, cup upon
each morning.

All this is God,
right here in my pea-green house
each morning
and I mean,
though often forget,
to give thanks,
to faint down by the kitchen table
in a prayer of rejoicing
as the holy birds at the kitchen window
peck into their marriage of seeds.

So while I think of it,

let me paint a thank-you on my palm
for this God, this laughter of the morning,
lest it go unspoken.
The joy that isn't shared, I've heard,
dies young.
–Anne Sexton

— 10 —

WE WILL MEET AGAIN TOMORROW

This body is not me.
I am not limited by this body.
I am life without boundaries.
I have never been born,
and I have never died.

Look at the ocean and the sky filled with stars,
manifestations from my wondrous true mind.

Since before time, I have been free.
Birth and death are only doors through which we pass,
sacred thresholds on our journey.
Birth and death are a game of hide-and-seek.

So laugh with me,
hold my hand,
let us say good-bye,
say good-bye, to meet again soon.

We meet today.
We will meet again tomorrow.
We will meet at the source every moment.
We meet each other in all forms of life.
—Thích Nhất Hạnh

— 11 —

THE BEAUTY IN EACH WAKING MOMENT

This day I pray for calm, for health, for clarity
For me and all others.
I pray for the wisdom to see the beauty of each waking moment.
Blessing be. Blessings for all.
—Cerridwen Greenleaf

— 12 —

NINE PURE GIFTS

We bathe your palms
In the showers of wine,
In the crook of the kindling,
In the seven elements,
In the sap of the tree,
In the milk of honey,

We place nine pure, choice gifts
In your clear beloved face:

149

The gift of form,
The gift of voice,
The gift of fortune,
The gift of goodness,
The gift of eminence,
The gift of charity,
The gift of integrity,
The gift of true nobility,
The gift of apt speech.

–Gaelic Song

— 13 —

THE VIEW FROM THE MOUNTAINTOP

And I've looked over.
And I've seen the promised land.
I may not get there with you.
But I want you to know tonight, that we
as a people will get to the promised land.
And I'm happy tonight.
I'm not worried about anything.
I'm not fearing any man.
Mine eyes have seen the glory of the coming of the Lord.

–Martin Luther King Jr., 1968

— 14 —

WHAT BRINGS US TO GRACE

Assailed by afflictions, we discover Dharma
And find the way to liberation. Thank you, evil forces!

When sorrows invade the mind, we discover Dharma
And find lasting happiness. Thank you, sorrows!

Through harm caused by spirits we discover Dharma
And find fearlessness. Thank you, ghosts and demons!

Through people's hate we discover Dharma
And find benefits and happiness. Thank you, those who hate us!

Through cruel adversity, we discover Dharma
And find the unchanging way. Thank you, adversity!

Through being impelled to by others, we discover Dharma
And find the essential meaning. Thank you, all who drive us on!

We dedicate our merit to you all, to repay your kindness.
—Gyalwa Longchenpa

— 15 —

LIFTED UP

Humble yourselves,
therefore, under God's mighty hand,
that he may lift you up in due time.
Cast all your anxiety on him
because he cares for you.
—1 Peter 5:6-7

— 16 —

SONGS OF THE HEART

At the still point of the universe
all that is not silence is song.
And all creation, hearing it, dances for joy.

The song of the universe is the song of life,
its rhythms defined by the cadence of time,
its beauty in its holy harmony.

The song is sung best when sung by the heart.
—Alfred V. Fedak

— 17 —

EMPTY YOUR HEART OF FEAR

Empty your heart of empty fears.
When you get yourself out of the way, I am there.
You can of yourself do nothing, but I can do all.
And I am in all.

Though you may not see the good, good is there, for
I am there. I am there because I have to be, because I am.

Only in Me does the world have meaning;
only out of Me does the world take form;
only because of Me does the world go forward.
I am the law on which the movement of the stars

and the growth of living cells are founded.
I am the love that is the law's fulfilling.

I am assurance.
I am peace.
I am oneness.
I am the law that you can live by.
I am the love that you can cling to.
I am your assurance.
I am your peace.
I am ONE with you.
I am.

Though you fail to find Me, I do not fail you.
Though your faith in Me is unsure,
My faith in you never wavers,
because I know you, because I love you.
Beloved, I AM there.
—James Dillet Freeman, 1947

— 18 —

EVERYTHING WILL BE ALRIGHT

I will breathe.
I will think of solutions.
I will not let my worry control me.
I will not let my stress level break me.
I will simply breathe.

And it will be okay.
Because I don't quit.
–Shayne McClendon

— 19 —

NATURE'S HEALING ENERGY

I am united with Source,
at one with all the most miraculous healing energies of Creation
and limitless in Wisdom, Appreciation, and Peace...
–Anonymous

— 20 —

A STEADFAST MIND

Humbly we pray that this mind
may be steadfast in us,
and that through these our hands,
and the hands of others
to whom thou shalt give the same spirit,
thou wilt vouchsafe to endow
the human family with new mercies.
–Francis Bacon, 1605

– 21 –

PRAYERS BRING HOPE

I pray for hope for those who feel none.
I pray for those in despair
to be lifted by the power of love.
I pray we all can be a part
of making this prayer come true.
–Steve Williamson

– 22 –

IT GETS BETTER

It gets better.
Stay in between my synapses
tap it out in Morse code
if need be.

It gets better.
Take me outside to look
at the birds flying in unison
taste the salty air
by the boundless ocean
feel the sand between clenched toes.

It gets better.
Take my mind off what
is too big for me
this thing I always dance around
and never mention.

That's why there is faith.
It's the bridge between
the impossible and the infinite.
Please get me and mine safely across.
–Ruth Williams

— 23 —

STAY ON THE HIGH ROAD

May the road rise up to meet you.
May the wind be always at your back.
May the sun shine warm upon your face,
the rains fall soft upon your fields, and until we meet again,
may God hold you in the palm of His hand.
–Irish Blessing

— 24 —

REJOICE IN POSITIVE THINGS

May we practice kindness day and night,
forever, not only towards friends, but also to
strangers, and especially to the enemy;
not only towards human beings,
but also to animals and other beings
who want happiness and don't want to suffer.

May we constantly enjoy our lives by rejoicing.

May we constantly enjoy happiness
by rejoicing in all the positive things that bring
benefit to others and to ourselves.
And may we especially rejoice when we see
all the good things that happen to others.

May we develop patience to achieve all happiness,
temporal and ultimate, and to bring that
happiness to others; not only to our family,
but to all sentient beings.

May we develop all the sixteen human qualities,
an understanding which makes our lives different.

May we become skilled in not harming sentient beings,
and may we become only the source of happiness
for sentient beings, like sunshine.

May we practice contentment.

May we learn contentment and satisfaction
May we learn to enjoy contentment,
which brings great freedom into our lives
and brings us so much happiness.
May we be an example to the world.

May we practice these good qualities,
and when somebody abuses or harms us,
may we immediately forgive them.
In daily life, when we make mistakes and harm others,
may we immediately ask forgiveness.

May we be able to develop courage
to be an inspiring example
and to be of benefit in so many ways for
the happiness of others, not only for ourselves.
—Lama Zopa Rinpoche

— 25 —

PRAYER FOR TOLERANCE

O! Thou God of all beings, of all worlds, and of all times,
We pray that the little differences in our clothes,
in our inadequate languages,
in our ridiculous customs,
in our imperfect laws,
in our illogical opinions,
in our ranks and conditions which
are so disproportionately important to us
and so meaningless to you,
that these small variations
that distinguish those atoms that we call men,
one from another,
may not be signals of hatred and persecution!
—Voltaire

– 26 –

SIT STILL

Blessed sister, holy mother,
spirit of the fountain, spirit of the garden,
Suffer us not to mock ourselves with falsehood
Teach us to care and not to care
Teach us to sit still
Even among these rocks,
Our peace in His will
And even among these rocks
Sister, mother
And spirit of the river, spirit of the sea,
Suffer me not to be separated
And let my cry come unto Thee.
–T.S. Eliot, 1927

– 27 –

STAY OPEN TO HAPPINESS

Let us pray for all to be happy,
to love one another,
to help each other,
to gain wisdom,
for all to receive god's blessings,
to break free from the illusion
that is distracting us from our true nature.

159

No one shall go hungry,
no one will suffer,
abundance is with everyone
and all negativity shall be removed!
—Brian Abiraj

– 28 –

SEE THE GRACE; SEE THE GOODNESS

Day by day,
Let me see the grace
Day by day,
Let me see the way

Day by day,
Let me see the beauty
Let me hear the music
Day by day,
Let me see the way

Day by day,
Let me see the goodness
Let me feel the love
Inspire me to kindness
Day by day,
Let me see the way

Let me see the grace
Let me see the way
—Hans Van Rostenberghe

— 29 —

HAVE A COMPASSIONATE HEART

Let us see one another through eyes
enlightened by understanding and compassion.

Release us from judgment so we can receive the stories
of our sisters and brothers with respect and attention.

Open our hearts to the cries of a suffering world
and the healing melodies of peace and justice for all creation.

Empower us to be instruments of justice
and equality everywhere.
—Jean Shinoda Bolen, *The Millionth Circle*

— 30 —

JUST KEEP PRAYING

Pray inwardly, even if you do not enjoy it.
It does good, though you feel nothing.
Yes, even though you think you are doing nothing.
—Julian of Norwich, 1373

— 31 —

A SMALL PRAYER FOR THOSE WITH DEPRESSION

Then we pray for many who are depressed
Now hurry little prayer, be on your way
So God can answer them this very day
Now bless us, God, in some small way
So we can know you heard us pray.

Amen.

–Alta Morgan

PRAYERS FOR PEACE OF MIND

"Be where you are, not where you think you should be."
—*Unknown*

"When I said, 'My foot is slipping,' your unfailing love, Lord, supported me. When anxiety was great within me, your consolation brought me joy."
—*Psalm 94:18–19*

"Therefore do not be anxious about tomorrow, for tomorrow will be anxious for itself. Sufficient for the day is its own trouble."
—*Matthew 6:34*

"Feel what you need to feel and then let it go. Do not let it consume you."
—*Dhiman*

"There is only one thing that makes a dream impossible to achieve: the fear of failure."
—*Paulo Coelho*

MINDFULNESS PRACTICE: JOYFUL CHOICES

This is your life; only you can truly control your choices, and choosing thankfulness and happiness is the best way to achieve being a good to yourself as well as the world. Here are some suggestions for how you can ensure simple joy in your life:

- Be the best you can be by your own standards

- Surround yourself with people who inspire you and make you feel good

- Focus on what you have, not what you lack

- Optimism trumps pessimism every time!

- Smile often and genuinely

- Be honest, to yourself and to others

- Help others

- Embrace your past, live in the present, and look forward for what is yet to come

AUGUST

MEDITATIONS FOR
MOVING FORWARD

"The belonging you seek is not behind you—it is ahead."

   —*Maz Kanata, Star Wars: The Force Awakens*

"Will this matter a year from now?"

   —*Unknown*

"What is coming is better than what has gone."

   —*Janice Johns*

"You can't go back and change the beginning, but you can stay where you are and change the ending."

   —*C.S. Lewis*

"Once you realize you deserve a bright future, letting go of your dark past is the best choice you will ever make."

   —*Roy T. Bennett*

— 1 —

YOU MADE IT TO HERE!

A year ago,
you did not know today.
You did not know
how you'd make it here.
But you made it here.
By grade, you made it here.
—Morgan Harper Nichols

— 2 —

MAKE THE BEST OF IT

For what it's worth:
it's never too late,
or in my case, too early,
to be whoever you want to be.
There's no time limit,
start whenever you want.
You can change or stay the same,
there are no rules to this thing.
We can make the best or the worst of it.
I hope you make the best of it.
I hope you see things that startle you.
I hope you feel things you've never felt before.

I hope you meet people who have a different point of view.
I hope you live a life you're proud of, and if you're not,
I hope you have the courage to start over again.
—F. Scott Fitzgerald

— 3 —
HOLD TO HOPE

Hope is the thing with feathers
that perches in the soul
and sings the tunes
without the words and never stops at all
—Emily Dickinson

— 4 —
DO NOT DWELL ON THE PAST

Forget the former things;
do not dwell on the past.
See, I am doing a new thing!
Now it springs up;
do you not perceive it?
I am making a way in the wilderness
and streams in the wasteland.
—Isaiah 43:18-19

— 5 —

FIND SOMETHING BETTER IN YOUR FUTURE

A very wise man once told me
that you can't look back–
you just have to put the past behind you,
and find something better in your future.

–Jodi Picoult

— 6 —

DON'T LOOK BACK

Make it a rule of life never to regret
and never to look back.
Regret is an appalling waste of energy;
you can't build on it;
it's only good for wallowing in.

–Katherine Mansfield

— 7 —

WALK RIGHT THROUGH THE DOOR

I've made tons of mistakes over the past years,
but if there's anything I've done well,
if I see an opportunity,
or if I see God moving

or going in a direction
or opening a door for me,
I try to take it;
I try not to hesitate.
—Shaun King

— 8 —

THE LESSON IN LETTING GO

You will find that it is necessary to let things go;
simply for the reason that they are heavy.
So let them go, let go of them.
I tie no weights to my ankles.
—C. JoyBell C.

— 9 —

LIGHT THE LIGHT OF A NEW IDEA

We light the light of a new idea.
It is the light of our coming together.
It is the light of our growing;
to know new things,
to see new beauty,
to feel new love.
—Unitarian Invocation

— 10 —

HEALING BODY, HEART, AND SOUL

Beloved Lord, Almighty God,
Through the Rays of the Sun,
Through the Waves of the Air,
Through the All Pervading Life in Space;
Purify and Revivify Us
And we pray, heal our bodies, hearts, and souls.
Amen
— Piro-Murshid Hazrat Inayat Khan

— 11 —

FINDING PEACE IN THE RIVER OF TEARS

Blessed be the story-tellers, music-makers, and artists at life,
for they are the true light of the world.

Blessed be the tender-hearted who mourn and grieve
the wars we've fought, the lives we've lost,
may peace ride in on the river of their tears.
—Jan Phillips

— 12 —

RELEASING, RELAXING

I am releasing
everything that is not in harmony with
the Divine Light & Sound pattern of my Being,
& everything that is not in harmony with
the Divine Light & Sound pattern
of my Being is releasing me.
—True Alisandre

— 13 —

IN THIS TOGETHERNESS

I am one with mother earth.
I am one with everyone within the reach of my voice.
And, in this togetherness, we ask the divine
intelligence to eradicate all
negatives from our hearts, from our minds,
from our words, and from our actions.
And, so be it.
—Babatunde Olatunji

— 14 —

WEAVING WEBS OF CHANGE

Lady, weave your web of change
Bring the world to peace again

Let us all be kin together.
So Mote It Be.
—**Rowan Fairgrove**

— 15 —

WALK QUIETLY ON THAT BEAUTIFUL TRAIL

Your feet I walk
I walk with your limbs
I carry forth your body
For me your mind thinks
Your voice speaks for me
Beauty is before me
And beauty is behind me
Above and below me hovers the beautiful
I am surrounded by it
I am immersed in it
In my youth I am aware of it
And in old age I shall walk quietly
The beautiful trail.
—**Navajo Chant**

— 16 —

ALL THINGS CALM

You are the peace of all things calm
You are the place to hide from harm

You are the light that shines in dark
You are the heart's eternal spark
You are the door that's open wide
You are the guest who waits inside
You are the stranger at the door
You are the calling of the poor
You are my Lord and with me still
You are my love, keep me from ill
You are the light, the truth, the way
—Ancient Celtic Adoration

— 17 —

FAITH CAN MOVE A MOUNTAIN

A faintish journey do I make
As through this frazzled world I wind,
With heavy heart and weary steps,
But with determined mind.

Beseech I for a flicker of
The faith that can a mountain move,
And hold that tenet close to me,
Believing where I cannot prove.

The pow'r that comes when sinking low
To man who grasps for straw or rope,
Will clutch til has he breathe no more
For where there's life, there's hope.

If my good turn be given to

My fellow man's deficiency,
I'll try to share my lowly gifts
Of Faith and Hope and Charity.
—Anne Shannon Demarest

— 18 —

HAPPY, WELL, AND PEACEFUL

May I be happy, well, and peaceful.
May my parents, grandparents, and ancestors
be happy, well, and peaceful.
May my brothers and sisters, my spouse
and children, my grandchildren
and all future generations be happy, well, and peaceful.
May all my friends and all my enemies be happy.
May all human beings sharing the earth be happy.
May all forms of life, plants, animals,
birds, fish, and insects be happy.
May all sentient beings in the universe be happy.
May we all be free from suffering and pain.
May we all be free from attachment of
greed, anger, and ignorance.
May we all attain perfect peace and
happiness of Enlightenment through
Buddha's Wisdom and Compassion.
—Reverend T. Kenjitsu Nakagaki

— 19 —

OUR PEACE

If we are peaceful,
if we are happy,
we can smile,
and everyone in our family,
our entire society,
will benefit from our peace.
– Thích Nhất Hạnh

— 20 —

SLOW DOWN

Tethered to our smartphones, we are too caught up and distracted to take the time necessary to sort through complexity or to locate submerged purpose. In our urgent rush to get "there," we are going everywhere but being nowhere. Far too busy managing with transactive speed, we rarely step back to lead with transformative significance.
–Kevin Cashman

— 21 —

MOMENTS OF CLARITY

I don't personally believe in
an arrived state of enlightenment.
I feel that being human
is a constant practice of return.
We have moments of clarity,
and then we're confused.
We have incredibly sensitive periods
of being awake and then we're numb.
Being human is a very universal
and a very personal practice of learning
how to return when we can't get access
to what we know.

–Mark Nepo

— 22 —

BE AT HOME IN YOUR OWN SKIN

It's not that God, the environment,
and other people cannot help us to be happy
or find satisfaction.
It's just that our happiness,
satisfaction, and our understanding,
even of God,
will be no deeper than our capacity
to know ourselves inwardly,
to encounter the world

from the deep comfort
that comes from being
at home in one's own skin,
from an intimate familiarity
with the ways of one's own mind and body.
–Jon Kabat-Zinn

— 23 —

PRAYER IS DOING

Prayer is not asking.
Prayer is putting oneself in the hands of God,
at his disposition,
and listening to his voice in the depths of our hearts.
–Mother Teresa

— 24 —

MIND YOUR LIFE

On the day when
the weight deadens
on your shoulders
and you stumble,
may the clay dance
to balance you.

And when your eyes
freeze behind
the grey window
and the ghost of loss
gets into you,
may a flock of colours,
indigo, red, green,
and azure blue
come to awaken in you
a meadow of delight.

When the canvas frays
in the currach of thought
and a stain of ocean
blackens beneath you,
may there come across the waters
a path of yellow moonlight
to bring you safely home.

May the nourishment of the earth be yours,
may the clarity of light be yours,
may the fluency of the ocean be yours,
may the protection of the ancestors be yours.
And so may a slow
wind work these words
of love around you,
an invisible cloak
to mind your life.

—John O'Donohue, *Echoes of Memory*

— 25 —

BATHE IN THE RIVER OF HEALING

For those who have no voice,
we ask you to speak.
For those who feel unworthy,
we ask you to pour your love out
in waterfalls of tenderness.
For those who live in pain,
we ask you to bathe them
in the river of your healing.
For those who are lonely, we ask
you to keep them company.
For those who are depressed,
we ask you to shower upon them
the light of hope.

–Maya Angelou

— 26 —

CLEANSE YOUR MIND

Thus it is our own mind
that should be established in all the Roots of the Good;
it is our own mind
that should be soaked by the rain of truth;
it is our own mind
that should be purified from all obstructive qualities;

it is our own mind
that should be made vigorous by energy.
—Gandavyuha Sutra

— 27 —

ARISE BEAUTIFUL AND FREE

May we love ever more.
May we motivate ourselves to committed love in Action.
May we motivate ourselves to live the
life we wish to see in the world.
May we be the transformation we wish to see in the world.
From the inside out...
From the roots branching upwards...
From the heart
to thought
to word
to action.
Through life's trials and hardships
we can arise beautiful and free.
—Julia Butterfly Hill

— 28 —

HEAL WHERE YOU ARE BROKEN

Let the rain come and wash away
the ancient grudges, the bitter hatreds

held and nurtured over generations.
Let the rain wash away the memory
of the hurt, the neglect.
Then let the sun come out and
fill the sky with rainbows.
Let the warmth of the sun heal us
wherever we are broken.
Let it burn away the fog so that
we can see each other clearly.
So that we can see beyond labels,
beyond accents, gender or skin color.
Let the warmth and brightness
of the sun melt our selfishness.
So that we can share the joys and
feel the sorrows of our neighbors.
And let the light of the sun
be so strong that we will see all
people as our neighbors.
Let the earth, nourished by rain,
bring forth flowers
to surround us with beauty.
And let the mountains teach our hearts
to reach upward to heaven.
Amen.

–Rabbi Harold Kushner

— 29 —

WHERE THERE IS SADNESS, LET THERE BE JOY

Lord, make me an instrument of Thy peace;
where there is hatred, let me sow love;
where there is injury, pardon;
where there is doubt, faith;
where there is despair, hope;
where there is darkness, light;
and where there is sadness, joy.
O Divine Master,
grant that I may not so much seek to be consoled as to console;
to be understood, as to understand;
to be loved, as to love;
for it is in giving that we receive,
it is in pardoning that we are pardoned,
and it is in dying that we are born to eternal life.
Amen.
–St. Francis of Assisi

— 30 —

BE IN BALANCE

The best and safest thing
is to keep a balance in your life,
acknowledge the great powers around us and in us.
If you can do that, and live that way,
you are really a wise man.
–Euripides

— 31 —

YOU MUST DO THE THING YOU
THINK YOU CANNOT DO

You gain strength, courage, and confidence
by every experience in which you really
stop to look fear in the face.
You are able to say to yourself, "I have lived through this horror.
I can take the next thing that comes along."
You must do the thing you think you cannot do.

–Eleanor Roosevelt

FACE FORWARD

"Whatever comes, let it come; what
stays, let stay; what goes, let go."
—*Papaji*

"It is important that we forgive ourselves
for making mistakes. We need to learn
from our errors and move forward."
—*Steve Maraboli*

"The longer we keep looking back in the rearview
mirror, it takes away from everything that's coming."
—*Dan Quinn*

"You've always had the power my dear,
you just had to learn it for yourself."
—*Glinda, The Wizard of Oz*

"The only person you are destined to become
is the person you decide to be."
—*Ralph Waldo Emerson*

"Life moves on and so should we."
—*Spencer Johnson*

ONE MINUTE RETREAT PRACTICES

You can meditate for as long or as little as you want. Do you only have a few minutes to meditate on your break? Then meditate for two minutes. Do you want to meditate for an hour before or after work? Meditate for an hour. Meditation is ultimately for your well-being, so you get to decide how long you do it.

Walking the Labyrinth—A Path of Grace to the Inner Self

At the Grace Cathedral on California Street in San Francisco, scholar Lauren Artress oversaw the installation of not one but two labyrinths. Sue Patton Thoele, author of *The Woman's Book of Soul*, invited me to go there one fine day a few years ago. I remember squeezing it into my schedule, feeling hurried, and hoping it would not take more than half an hour or so. I am a bit embarrassed to admit this, but I know I am not the only busy life-juggler who has found herself surprised by the Sacred.

When we got there, a magnificent stillness permeated the entire cathedral. We chose the indoor labyrinth instead of the outdoor one, as there was a distinct chill in the foggy air that day. We read the simple instructions and, as told, removed our shoes to tread the path in bare or stocking feet. For my part, I had already begun to calm down, thanks to the peaceful atmosphere. As I walked in the light of the stained-glass shadows, my schedule started to seem petty. Suddenly it seemed as if I could give this just a little more time.

Sue, an experienced labyrinth walker, had gone ahead and seemed to be in a reverie, as did the tourists, students, and random folks who populated the nave. I checked the instructions again just to make sure I performed my barefoot ritual "correctly."

As I began, thoughts skittered through my head, and I had to struggle to focus and be in the now. With no small amount of effort, I was able to have an authentic experience. As I walked the winding path, a replica of the labyrinth on the floor of Chartres Cathedral, I felt a growing excitement. This was meaningful; perhaps there was hope even for me and my over-busy "monkey mind." My breathing relaxed, and I had a growing sense that I was going somewhere. When I reached the center of the labyrinth, I looked up at the soaring high ceiling of Grace Cathedral. At that exact moment, the sun struck a stained-glass window and a golden shaft of light shone directly upon me. I was mystified, and a beaming Sue, having completed her walk, noticed what was happening to me. I studied the window to see if there was any kind of symbol from which to draw further meaning. To my astonishment, the sun had lit up a window that contained the medieval tableau of a sword in a rock. As a lapsed medieval scholar, I immediately recognized Excalibur of the famous Arthurian legend. Tears came into my eyes, and I realized this was a message. I had often felt a bit guilty for not completing my master's degree in medieval studies. At that moment, I knew I had to complete that quest. One of my specializations was the Arthurian saga, and here, in no uncertain terms, Arthur's sword had spoken to me as I stood in the center of the labyrinth. Exhilarated, I retraced my steps, and returned the same way I had entered, now brimming with joy. Now, I truly understand what it means to be "illuminated."

Walking Meditation–How to Walk the Labyrinth

The labyrinth represented wholeness to the ancients, combining the circle and the spiral in one archetypal image. The labyrinth is unicursal, meaning there is only one path, both in and out. Put simply, it is a journey into the self, into your own center, and back into the world again. As a prayer and meditation tool, labyrinths are peerless; they awaken intuition.

Do your best to relax before you enter. Deep breaths will help a great deal. If you have a specific question in mind, think it or whisper it to yourself. You will meet others on the pilgrim's path as you are walking; simply step aside and let them continue on their journey as you do the same. The three stages of the labyrinth walk are as follows:

Purgation: Here is where you free your mind of all worldly concerns. It is a release, a letting go. Still your mind and open your heart. Shed worries and emotion as you step out on the path.

Illumination: When you have come to the center, you are in the place of illumination. Here, you should stay as long as you feel the need to pray and meditate. In this quiet center, the heart of the labyrinth, you will receive messages from the Divine or from your own higher power. Illumination can also come from deep inside yourself.

Union: This last phase is where you will experience union with the divine. Lauren Artress says that as you "walk the labyrinth, you become more empowered to find and do the work you feel your soul requires."

Use this walking meditation to become one with yourself and find peace within. May you use this learned tranquility to better participate in other rituals that focus on important aspects of your life.

SEPTEMBER

FINDING THE
STILLNESS WITHIN

"Feelings are just visitors, let them come and go."
  —*Mooji*

"It was her habit to build laughter out of inadequate materials."
  —*John Steinbeck, The Grapes of Wrath*

"The mind is like water. When it's turbulent, it's difficult to see. When it's calm, everything becomes clear."
  —*Prasad Mahes*

"Have a heart that never hardens, a temper that never tires, and a touch that never hurts."
  —*Charles Dickens*

"You can't always control what goes on outside, but you can always control what goes on inside."
  —*Wayne Dyer*

— 1 —

HYMN TO TIME

Time says "Let there be"
every moment and instantly
there is space and the radiance
of each bright galaxy.

And eyes beholding radiance.
And the gnats' flickering dance.
And the seas' expanse.
And death, and chance.

Time makes room
for going and coming home
and in time's womb
begins all ending.

Time is being and being
time, it is all one thing,
the shining, the seeing,
the dark abounding.
—Ursula Le Guin

— 2 —

THE THINGS THAT MAKE THEM THE BEST

The best people possess a feeling for beauty,
the courage to take risks,
the discipline to tell the truth,
the capacity for sacrifice.
—**Ernest Hemingway**

— 3 —

YOU CAN HEAL YOURSELF

You have the power to heal yourself,
and you need to know that.
We think so often that we are helpless
but we're not.
We always have the power of our minds.
Claim and consciously use your power.
—**Louise Hay**

— 4 —

YOU SHALL OVERCOME

Within ourselves,
there are voices
that provide us with all the
answers that we need
to heal our deepest wounds,

193

to transcend our limitations,
to overcome our obstacles
or challenges, and to see
where our soul is longing to go.
—**Debbie Ford**

— 5 —

IF YOU LET GO A LOT, YOU'LL HAVE A LOT OF PEACE

Do everything with a mind that lets go.
Do not expect any praise or reward.
If you let go a little,
you will have a little peace.
If you let go a lot,
you will have a lot of peace.
If you let go completely,
you will know complete peace and freedom.
Your struggles with the world will have come to an end.
—**Achaan Chah, Thai Buddhist Monk, 1955**

— 6 —

DON'T BRING SUFFERING ONTO YOURSELF

We often add to our pain and suffering
by being overly sensitive,

overreacting to minor things,
and sometimes taking things too personally.
—Dalai Lama

— 7 —

STAND IN YOUR POWER

I stand in my own power now,
the questions of permission
that I used to choke on
for my every meal
now dead in a fallen heap,
and when they tell me that I will fall,
I nod. I will fall, I reply, and
my words are a whisper
my words are a howl
I will fall, I say,
and the tumbling will be all my own.
The skinned palms and oozing knees are holy wounds,
stigmata of my She.
I will catch my own spilled blood,
and not a drop will be wasted.
—Beth Morey

– 8 –

IT IS FINISHED IN BEAUTY

In the house made of dawn.
In the story made of dawn.
On the trail of dawn.
O, Talking God.
His feet, my feet, restore.
His limbs, my limbs, restore.
His body, my body, restore.
His voice, my voice, restore.
His plumes, my plumes, restore.
With beauty before him, with beauty before me.
With beauty behind him, with beauty behind me.
With beauty above him, with beauty above me.
With beauty below him, with beauty below me.
With beauty around him, with beauty around me.
With pollen beautiful in his voice,
with pollen beautiful in my voice.
It is finished in beauty.
It is finished in beauty.
In the house of evening light.
From the story made of evening light.
On the trail of evening light.

–Navajo Chant

— 9 —

BE THE MEANING OF THE POEM

I am the wind on the sea.

I am the ocean wave.

I am the sound of the billows.

I am the seven-horned stag.

I am the hawk on the cliff.

I am the dewdrop in sunlight.

I am the fairest of flowers.

I am the raging boar.

I am the salmon in the deep pool.

I am the lake on the plain.

I am the meaning of the poem.

I am the point of the spear.

I am the god who makes fire in the head.

Who levels the mountain?

Who speaks the age of the moon?

Who has been where the sun sleeps?

Who, if not I?

—*The Song of Amergin*, **Celtic poetic invocation**

— 10 —

TURN OF A YEAR

This is regret: or a ferret. Snuffling,
stunted, a snout full of snow.

As the end of day shuffles down
the repentant scurry and swarm—

an unstable contrition is born.
Bend down. Look into the lair.

Where newborn pieties spark and strike
I will make my peace as a low bulb

burnt into a dent of snow. A cloth to keep me
from seeping. Light crumpled over a hole.

Why does the maker keep me awake?
He must want my oddments, their glow.

—Joan Houlihan

— 11 —

ARRIVE AT TRANQUILITY

We fluctuate long
between love and hatred
before we can arrive at tranquility.

—Peter Abelard

— 12 —

PRAYERS COME TRUE

I pray for hope for those who feel none.
I pray for those in despair
to be lifted by the power of love.

I pray we all can be a part
of making this prayer come true.
–Steve Williamson

— 13 —

LOVE IS OUR REFUGE

Love is our refuge; only with mine eye
Can I behold the snare, the pit, the fall:
His habitation high is here, and nigh,
His arm encircles me, and mine, and all.

O make me glad for every scalding tear,
For hope deferred, ingratitude, disdain!
Wait, and love more for every hate, and fear
No ill–since God is good, and loss is gain.

Beneath the shadow of His mighty wing;
In that sweet secret of the narrow way,
Seeking and finding, with the angels sing:
"Lo, I am with you always"–watch and pray.

No snare, no fowler, pestilence or pain;
No night drops down upon the troubled breast,
When heaven's aftersmile earth's tear-drops gain,
And mother finds her home and heavenly rest.

–Mary Baker Eddy

— 14 —

OUR HUMAN COMMUNITY

For this fragile planet earth,
its times and tides, its sunsets and seasons:

We give thanks this day.

For the joy of human life,
its wonders and surprises, its hopes and achievements:

We give thanks this day.

For our human community,
our common past and future hope,
our oneness transcending all separation,
our capacity to work for peace and justice in
the midst of hostility and oppression:

We give thanks this day.

—O. Eugene Pickett

— 15 —

LIGHTS OF CLARITY

Fire of the Spirit,
life of the lives of creatures,
Spiral of sanctity,
Bond of all natures,
glow of charity,
lights of clarity,

taste of sweetness to the fallen,
be with us and hear us.
—Hildegarde of Bingen

— 16 —

ONE MOMENT AT A TIME

Living one day at a time,
Enjoying one moment at a time,
Accepting hardship as a pathway to peace,
Taking, as Jesus did,
This sinful world as it is,
Not as I would have it,
Trusting that You will make all things right,
If I surrender to Your will,
So that I may be reasonably happy in this life,
And supremely happy with You forever in the next.
Amen.
—Reinhold Niebuhr

— 17 —

THOUGH I MAY STUMBLE

As the rain hides the stars,
as the autumn mist
hides the hills,

201

as the clouds veil
the blue of the sky, so
the dark happenings of my lot
hide the shining of thy face from me.
Yet, if I may hold thy hand in the darkness,
it is enough, since I know,
that though I may stumble in my going,
Thou dost not fall.
—Scottish Blessing

— 18 —

SHELTER FROM DANGER

Let me not pray to be sheltered from dangers
but to be fearless in facing them.

Let me not beg for the stilling of my pain
but for the heart to conquer it.

Let me not look for allies in life's battlefield
but to my own strength.

Let me not crave in anxious fear to be saved
but hope for the patience to win my freedom.
—Rabindranath Tagore

— 19 —

DO NOT WORRY ABOUT YOUR LIFE

Then Jesus said to his disciples:
"Therefore I tell you,
do not worry about your life,
what you will eat;
or about your body,
what you will wear.
For life is more than food,
and the body more than clothes."
—Luke 12:22-34

— 20 —

BE CALM IN YOUR HEART

Peace.
It does not mean to be in a place
where there is no noise,
trouble, or hard work.
It means to be in the midst
of those things and still be calm in your heart.
—Unknown

— 21 —
QUIETNESS

Help me to find my happiness
in my acceptance of what is my purpose
in friendly eyes, in work well done,
in quietness born of trust.
And most of all
in the awareness of spirit in my being.
–Hebridean Celtic Blessing

— 22 —
TAKE CARE

Feelings, whether of compassion or irritation, should be
welcomed, recognized, and treated on an absolutely equal basis;
because both are ourselves. The tangerine I am eating is me.
The mustard greens I am planting are me. I plant with all my
heart and mind. I clean this teapot with the kind of attention
I would have were I giving the baby Buddha or Jesus a bath.
Nothing should be treated more carefully than anything else.
–Thích Nhất Hạnh

— 23 —
BOUNDARIES ARE BEAUTIFUL

Love yourself enough to set boundaries.
Your time and energy are precious.

You get to choose how you use it.
You teach people how to treat you
by deciding what you will and won't accept.
—Anna Taylor

— 24 —

GROWING IN AWARENESS

One does not become enlightened
by imagining figures of light
but by making the darkness conscious.
—C. G. Jung

— 25 —

BE A BUDDHA

So to be a human being is to be a Buddha.
Buddha nature is just another name for human nature,
our true human nature. Thus even though
you do not do anything,
you are actually doing something.
You are expressing yourself.
You are expressing your true nature.
Your eyes will express;
your voice will express;
your demeanor will express.
The most important thing is to express your true nature

205

in the simplest, most adequate way
and to appreciate it in the smallest existence
–Shunryu Suzuki

— 26 —

THE CEREMONY

The ceremony of lifting up our hands in prayer
is designed to remind us that we are far removed from God,
unless our thoughts rise upward.
–John Calvin

— 27 —

BEING HERE NOW

It's like wearing gloves every time we touch something,
and then, forgetting we chose to put them on,
we complain that nothing feels quite real.
Our challenge each day is not to get dressed
to face the world but to unglove ourselves
so that the doorknob feels cold and the car handle
feels wet and the kiss goodbye feels like
the lips of another being, soft and unrepeatable.
–Mark Nepo

— 28 —

THE SERENITY OF PRAYER

For me, it is essential
to have the inner peace
and serenity of prayer
in order to listen
to the silence of God,
which speaks to us,
in our personal life
and the history of our times,
of the power of love.
—Adolfo Perez Esquivel

— 29 —

A QUIET, CALM SPIRIT

Never be in a hurry;
do everything quietly
and in a calm spirit.
Do not lose your inner peace
for anything whatsoever,
even if your whole world seems upset.
—Saint Francis de Sales

— 30 —
I WILL LOVE YOU GENTLY

If I must worry about how
I will live in my old age
without wealth
I would be without health now
and how can I live to be
old?

If I must worry about how
I will live in my old age
without love
I would be without dreams now
and how can I go on living
another day?

Allow me to sit in the sun
and listen to the sky.
I will love you gently.

–Chungmi Kim

REMINDERS OF BALANCE

"Look well into thyself; there is a source of strength which will always spring up if thou wilt always look."
—*Marcus Aurelius*

"My faith helps me understand that circumstances don't dictate my happiness, my inner peace."
—*Denzel Washington*

"Whatever the mind can conceive and believe, it can achieve."
—*Napoleon Hill*

"If thou wilt make a man happy, add not unto his riches but take away from his desires."
—*Epicurus*

"Things work out best for those who make the best of how things work out."
—*John Wooden*

"If you want to conquer the anxiety of life, live in the moment, live in the breath."
—*Amit Ray*

PRACTICE OF QUIETUDE

Inward-Focused Meditative Walk

The inward-focused meditative walk is intended to use the movement of your body while walking as a focus for your mind. I like to do it when I've been sitting still all day, so sitting more to meditate is difficult and distraction filled.

Begin by standing still in a safe location. Take a deep breath in and allow your eyes to slowly close as you breathe out, then breathe normally. Focus on the weight of your body transferring to the ground. Notice the small movements you normally make without thinking, the shifts that help you maintain balance. Once you feel grounded, slowly open your eyes and take your first step. Walk normally—not too slow, not too fast. As you begin walking, focus on the sensations of your feet as they meet the ground. Notice how your weight transfers, the textures that rub against each foot as you take a step. When you're ready, slowly bring your focus upward to your legs. Notice how your ankles and knees are bending, how your leg muscles expand and contract. How the fabric around your legs feels as it shifts along with your pace. When you're ready, raise your focus to your torso. Pay attention to the small twists and turns it makes as you're walking, to the weight of your top on your body. Over time, expand this focus to include your arms. Are they swinging? If so, how far? Do they feel heavy or light? After you feel content with how you have acknowledged and appreciated each part of your body, shift your focus to your head. Notice how you're holding it and release any tension in your neck or in the rest of your body. Allow yourself to relax and enjoy the walk. When you're ready, gently let go of your inward focus and continue with your day.

OCTOBER

CALMING
CONTEMPLATIONS

"Whatever you did today is enough. Whatever you felt today is valid. Whatever you thought today isn't to be judged. Repeat the above each day."
   —*Brittany Burgunder*

"Gratitude and esteem are good foundations of affection."
   —*Jane Austen*

"When you arise in the morning, think of what a precious privilege it is to be alive—to breathe, to think, to enjoy, to love."
   —*Marcus Aurelius*

"I have found that worry and irritation vanish the moment when I open my mind to the many blessings that I possess."
   —*Dale Carnegie*

"It is impossible to feel grateful and depressed in the same moment."
   —*Naomi Williams*

— 1—

UP-HILL

Does the road wind up-hill all the way?
>Yes, to the very end.
Will the day's journey take the whole long day?
>From morn to night, my friend.

But is there for the night a resting-place?
>A roof for when the slow dark hours begin.
May not the darkness hide it from my face?
>You cannot miss that inn.

Shall I meet other wayfarers at night?
>Those who have gone before.
Then must I knock, or call when just in sight?
>They will not keep you standing at that door.

Shall I find comfort, travel-sore and weak?
>Of labour you shall find the sum.
Will there be beds for me and all who seek?
>Yea, beds for all who come.

>—Christina Rossetti 1830-1894

— 2 —

THE STILLNESS OF THE STARS GUARD YOU

May the peace of the tallest mountain
and the peace of the smallest stone
be your peace.
May the stillness of the stars watch over you.
May the everlasting music of the wave lull you to rest.
—Celtic Blessing Prayer

— 3 —

STORMS ARE GONE

How calm, how beautiful comes on
The stilly hour, when storms are gone!
When warring winds have died away,
And clouds, beneath the glancing ray,
Melt off, and leave the land and sea
Sleeping in bright tranquillity.
—Thomas Moore

— 4 —

PEACE, JOY AND SERENITY

Every breath we take,
every step we make,

can be filled with peace,
joy and serenity.
—Thích Nhất Hạnh

— 5 —

THE HAPPINESS OF YOUR LIFE

The happiness of your life
depends upon the quality of your thoughts;
therefore, guard accordingly,
and take care that you entertain
no notions unsuitable to virtue
and reasonable nature.
—Marcus Aurelius

— 6 —

LIFE AFTER MISTAKES

I had the chance
to make every possible mistake
and figure out a way to recover from it.
Once you realize there is life after mistakes,
you gain a self-confidence that never goes away.
—Bob Schieffer

— 7 —

PRAYER FOR HEALTH AND HAPPINESS

Om sarvetra sukhinah santu sarve santu niramayah.
Sarve bhadrani pasyantu ma kascid duhkhamapnuyat
Om shantih shantih shantih
Oh Almighty! May everybody be happy!
May all be free from ailments!
May we see what is auspicious!
May no one be subject to miseries!
Oh Almighty! May there be a Peace! Peace! Peace! Everywhere
–*The Rig-Veda*, India, 3700 BC

— 8 —

ALL HER PATHS ARE PEACE

Blessed are those who find wisdom,
those who gain understanding,
for she is more profitable than silver
and yields better returns than gold.
She is more precious than rubies;
nothing you desire can compare with her.
Long life is in her right hand;
in her left hand are riches and honor.
Her ways are pleasant ways,
and all her paths are peace.
She is a tree of life to those who take hold of her;
those who hold her fast will be blessed.
–**Proverbs 3:13–18**

— 9 —

KEEP LOOKING FOR THE OPEN DOORS

When one door of happiness closes,
another opens,
but often we look so long
at the closed door
that we do not see the one
that has been opened for us.
—Helen Keller

— 10 —

QUIET CONFIDENCE

The Lord's justice will dwell in the desert,
his righteousness live in the fertile field.
The fruit of that righteousness will be peace;
its effect will be quietness and confidence forever.
—Isaiah 32:16–17

— 11 —

THE FIRST PEACE

The first peace, which is the most important, is that which comes
within the Souls of people when they realize their relationship,
their oneness with the universe and all its powers, and when

they realize at the center of the universe dwells the Great Spirit,
and that its center is really everywhere, it is within each of us.
—Black Elk

— 12 —

YOU THINK THEREFORE YOU ARE

It isn't what you have,
or who you are,
or where you are,
or what you are doing
that makes you happy or unhappy.
It is what you think about.
—Dale Carnegie

— 13 —

MY RELIGION IS KINDNESS

If you wish to experience peace, provide peace for another.
If you wish to know that you are safe, cause
another to know that they are safe.
If you wish to better understand seemingly
incomprehensible things,
help another to better understand.
If you wish to heal your own sadness or anger,
seek to heal the sadness or anger of another.

Those others are waiting for you now. They
are looking to you for guidance,
for help, for courage, for strength, for understanding,
and for assurance at this hour.
Most of all, they are looking to you for love.
My religion is very simple.
My religion is kindness.
–His Holiness the fourteenth Dalai Lama, 1981

— 14 —

FEEL THE FEAR AND DO IT ANYWAY

I learned that courage
was not the absence of fear,
but the triumph over it.
The brave man is not he
who does not feel afraid,
but he who conquers that fear.
–Nelson Mandela

— 15 —

THREE METHODS

By three methods we may learn wisdom:
First, by reflection, which is noblest;
Second, by imitation,
which is easiest;

and third by experience,
which is the bitterest.
–Confucius

– 16 –

LEAD US TO LIGHT AND TRUTH

Asatho Maa Sad Gamaya. Thamaso Maa Jyothir Gamaya.
Mrithyur Maa Amritham Gamaya. Om Shanti, Shanti, Shanti.

From untruth lead us to Truth. From darkness lead us to Light.
From death lead us to Immortality. Om Peace, Peace, Peace.
–Ancient Vedic Prayer

– 17 –

FINDING THE TREASURE WITHIN

Looking behind,
I am filled with gratitude.
Looking forward,
I am filled with vision.
Looking upwards,
I am filled with strength.
Looking within, I discover peace.
–Native American Proverb

— 18 —

SIMPLE IN ACTIONS AND THOUGHTS

Simplicity, patience, compassion.
These three are your greatest treasures.
Simple in actions and thoughts, you return to the source of being.
Patient with both friends and enemies,
you accord with the way things are.
Compassionate toward yourself,
you reconcile all beings in the world.

–Lao Tzu

— 19 —

CONNECT THE DOTS

You can't connect the dots looking forward;
you can only connect them looking backward.
So you have to trust that the dots
will somehow connect in your future.
You have to trust in something–
your gut, destiny, life, karma, whatever.
This approach has never let me down,
and it has made all the difference in my life.

–Steve Jobs

— 20 —

DEEP COMFORT

It's not that God,
the environment,
and other people
cannot help us
to be happy
or find satisfaction.
It's just that our happiness,
satisfaction, and our understanding,
even of God, will be no deeper
than our capacity
to know ourselves inwardly,
to encounter the world
from the deep comfort
that comes from being
at home in one's own skin,
from an intimate familiarity
with the ways
of one's own mind and body.
–Jon Kabat-Zinn

— 21 —

GOOD WILL HUNTING

Mindful self-compassion can be learned by anyone. It's the
practice of repeatedly evoking good will toward ourselves

especially when we're suffering—cultivating the same desire that
all living beings have to live happily and free from suffering.

—Christopher Germer

— 22 —

PUT IT INTO PRACTICE

Finally, brothers and sisters, whatever is true, whatever
is noble, whatever is right, whatever is pure, whatever is
lovely, whatever is admirable—if anything is excellent or
praiseworthy—think about such things. Whatever you have
learned or received or heard from me, or seen in me—put
it into practice. And the God of peace will be with you.

—Philippians 4:8-9

— 23 —

THIS IS YOUR LIFE

You have to remember one life, one death—this one!
To enter fully the day, the hour, the moment whether it appears
as life or death, whether we catch it on the inbreath or outbreath,
requires only a moment, this moment. And along with it all
the mindfulness we can muster, and each stage of our ongoing
birth, and the confident joy of our inherent luminosity.

—Stephen Levine

— 24 —

DON'T WASTE YOUR HAPPINESS

There is no beauty in sadness.
No honor in suffering.
No growth in fear.
No relief in hate.
It's just a waste of perfectly good happiness.
–Katerina Stoykova Klemer

— 25 —

WHAT IS DONE IN LOVE

It is good to love many things
for therein lies the true strength,
and whosoever loves much performs much,
and can accomplish much,
and what is done in love is well done.
–Vincent Van Gogh

— 26 —

JOY AND GOOD WILL AND SERENITY

As you cannot have a sweet and wholesome abode
unless you admit the air and sunshine freely into your rooms,
so a strong body

and a bright, happy, or serene countenance
can only result from the free admittance into the mind
of thoughts of joy and good will and serenity.
–James Allen

— 27 —

EACH PRESENT MOMENT

Start living right here,
in each present moment.
When we stop dwelling on the past
or worrying about the future,
we're open to rich sources of information
we've been missing out on–
information that can keep us
out of the downward spiral
and poised for a richer life.
–Mark Williams

— 28 —

FEEL YOURSELF BREATHING

What is the date? What is the time? Great, that's what
Now is. And every second, your "Now" changes. Because
all we have is Now. We are continuously living in the
Now. Not yesterday, not tomorrow, but Now. Today.

The present. And I need you to live in it. To truly
appreciate it. To breathe and feel yourself breathing.
–S.R. Crawford

— 29 —

A SECRET TO HEALTH AND HAPPINESS

To enjoy good health, to bring true happiness to
one's family, to bring peace to all, one must first
discipline and control one's own mind.
–Buddha

— 30 —

THE ART OF LIVING

The art of living...is neither careless drifting on the one hand
nor fearful clinging to the past on the other. It consists in
being sensitive to each moment, in regarding it as utterly new
and unique, in having the mind open and wholly receptive.
–Alan Watts

— 31 —

YET SHALL BE

Bliss in possession will not last;
Remember'd joys are never past;
At once the fountain, stream, and sea,
They were,–they are,–they yet shall be.
–James Montgomery

OTHER WAYS TO FIND YOUR ZEN

"Yesterday is history, tomorrow is a mystery, today is a gift of God, which is why we call it the present."
—*Bill Keane*

"It's been my experience that you can nearly always enjoy things if you make up your mind firmly that you will."
—*L.M. Montgomery*

"The most wasted of all days is one without laughter."
—*Nicolas Chamfort*

"What you feed your mind, will lead your life."
—*Kemi Sogunle*

"Mindfulness means being aware of how you're deploying your attention and making decisions about it, and not letting the tweet or the buzzing of your BlackBerry call your attention."

—*Howard Rheingold*

"The mind is just like a muscle—the more you exercise it, the stronger it gets and the more it can expand."

—*Idowu Koyenikan*

"The body benefits from movement, and the mind benefits from stillness."

—*Sakyong Mipham*

PRAYERFUL PRACTICE: MANTRA MEDITATION

Mantra meditation is intended to use sounds, words, and phrases to refocus you. I like to do mantra meditation when I can't seem to escape all of my thoughts and worries about the future or the past.

For this meditation, you must come up with a word or phrase that you will repeat over and over again. This will be your mantra. One of the traditional words used is "Ohm," but it could be anything, secular or non, spiritual or non. Remember, though, that the word, sound, or phrase you use will replace your thoughts, so it should be chosen carefully, as it will be your focus for the entirety of your meditation and perhaps even for a period afterwards.

Begin by sitting in a comfortable position. Take a deep breath in and let it out, slowly closing your eyes or allowing your visual focus to blur. Then begin your mantra. You can repeat it silently or murmur or whisper it quietly out loud. Focus all of your mind, all of your energy, on your mantra, allowing it to consume your every thought. You can do this a certain number of times, using a method to track your number that does not involve focusing on counting, such as moving beads along a necklace. Or, you can do this for a set amount of time, setting a non-obtrusive, mild timer that will alert you to when your meditation is finished. When you

231

are done, take a deep breath in, and as you let it out, allow yourself to refocus on the world around you and mindfully continue your day.

NOVEMBER

ATTITUDES OF
GRATITUDE

"Love is Love is Gratitude."

   —Brenda Knight

"Paying attention to and staying with finer and finer sensations within the body is one of the surest ways to steady the wandering mind."

   —Ravi Ravindra

"Mindfulness is deliberately paying full attention to what is happening around you—in your body, heart, and mind. Mindfulness is awareness without criticism or judgment."

   —Hab Chozen Bays

"Mindfulness has helped me succeed in almost every dimension of my life. By stopping regularly to look inward and become aware of my mental state, I stay connected to the source of my actions and thoughts and can guide them with considerably more intention."

   —Dustin Moskovitz

"Radiate boundless love towards the entire world."

—*Buddha*

"Sati-sampajanna ("Mindfulness and clear comprehension") should be examined carefully from the point of view of the centipede who could not walk when she thought about how she moved her limbs. And also from the point of view of absorption in, say artistic creation and detached observation of it. Absorption in piano playing or painting seems to be "successful" but detached observation or enjoyment of "my playing"...seems to have the centipede effect."

—*Nanamoli Thera*

"The most fundamental aggression to ourselves, the most fundamental harm we can do to ourselves, is to remain ignorant by not having the courage and the respect to look at ourselves honestly and gently."

—*Pema Chödrön*

235

— 1 —

THE KISS OF THE SUN

The greatest gift
I ever received
was the kiss of the sun
on the days where
I couldn't remember
how to make my own light.
—Unknown

— 2 —

SAFE FROM THE STORM

When the storm rages around me,
and I can hold on no more,
when the waves of fear engulf me
and I am weary, battered and sore,
take me then and steer me storm-tossed,
broken and afraid,
into the arms of your safe harbor safely home.
—Prayer to St. Benedict

— 3 —
WHAT COMES AFTER THE SADNESS

Dear God, After the sadness I didn't think I could ever be the same again. I was right. I now have qualities I never had before. I am more sensitive to the sorrows of others. I am more compassionate to the less fortunate. I appreciate deeply. I love more intensely. Thank You for giving me the wisdom that comes from life experiences. Amen.

–Martha Lynn, Harmony Hollow

— 4 —
DO NOT BE AFRAID

Fear not, for I am with you;
be not dismayed,
for I am your God;
I will strengthen you,
I will help you,
I will uphold you with my righteous right hand.

–Isaiah 41:10

— 5 —

WELCOME GOOD

Let gratitude be the pillow upon which you kneel to
say your nightly prayer. And let faith be the bridge
you build to overcome evil and welcome good.

–Maya Angelou

— 6 —

SIMPLE WISDOM

Act justly.
Love mercy.
Walk humbly.

–Micah 8:8

— 7 —

PEACE AND LOVE

We do not want riches
but we do want to train
our children right.
Riches would do us no good.
We could not take them
with us to the other world.
We do not want riches.
We want peace and love.

–Chief Red Cloud, Oglala Lakota

– 8 –

STRENGTH AND SHIELD

The Lord is my strength and my shield;
my heart trusts in him, and he helps me.
My heart leaps for joy,
and with my song I praise him.
–Psalm 28:7

– 9 –

TEND YOUR OWN GARDEN

Let us be grateful
to the people who make us happy;
they are the charming gardeners
who make our souls blossom.
–Marcel Proust

– 10 –

REMEMBER

Remember that the happiest people are not
those getting more, but those giving more.
–H. Jackson Brown, Jr.

— 11 —

EVERYTHING IS GOOD

For everything God created is good,
and nothing is to be rejected if it is received with thanksgiving,
because it is consecrated by the word of God and prayer.
–1 Timothy 4:4-5

— 12 —

A GRATEFUL HEART

God has two dwellings;
one in heaven,
and the other in a meek
and thankful heart.
–Izaak Walton

— 13 —

#BLESSED

The Lord bless you
and keep you;
the Lord make his face shine on you
and be gracious to you;

the Lord turn his face toward you
and give you peace.
–Numbers 6:24–26

— 14 —

TAP INTO WONDER

Rather than fretting about the past or worrying about the
future, the aim is to experience life as it unfolds moment by
moment. This simple practice is immensely powerful. As we
rush through our lives, mindfulness encourages us to stop
constantly striving for something new or better and to embrace
acceptance and gratitude. This allows us to tap into the joy and
wonder in our lives, and to listen to the wisdom of our hearts.
–Anna Barnes

— 15 —

THE THREE THINGS THAT MATTER

In the end, just three things matter:
How well we have lived
How well we have loved
How well we have learned to let go
–Jack Kornfield

241

— 16 —

CULTIVATE GRATITUDE

Cultivate the habit of being grateful for every good thing
that comes to you, and to give thanks continuously. And
because all things have contributed to your advancement,
you should include all things in your gratitude.

–Ralph Waldo Emerson

— 17 —

GIVE AND YOU SHALL RECEIVE

You will be enriched in every way
so that you can be generous on every occasion,
and through us your generosity will
result in thanksgiving to God.

–2 Corinthians 9:11

— 18 —

CROWDED KINDNESSES

Do not let the empty cup be your first teacher of the
blessings you had when it was full. Do not let a hard
place here and there in the bed destroy your rest. Seek,
as a plain duty, to cultivate a buoyant, joyous sense of
the crowded kindnesses of God in your daily life.

–Alexander Maclaren

— 19 —

DON'T LET WORRY GET IN THE WAY OF YOUR JOY

We speculate, dream, strategize, and plan for these
"conditions of happiness" we want to have in the future;
and we continually chase after that future, even while we
sleep. We may have fears about the future because we
don't know how it's going to turn out, and these worries
and anxieties keep us from enjoying being here now.

–Thích Nhất Hạnh

— 20 —

LIVE EACH LIFE AS IF IT WAS YOUR LAST

Perfection of character is this: to live each day as if it were
your last, without frenzy, without apathy, without pretense.

–Marcus Aurelius

— 21 —

STAY OPEN TO ABUNDANCE

When you are grateful, fear disappears and abundance appears.

–Tony Robbins

— 22 —
ENOUGH IS A GIFT

Be thankful for what you have; you'll end up
having more. If you concentrate on what you don't
have, you will never, ever have enough.

–Oprah Winfrey

— 23 —
CONTENTMENT

True happiness is to enjoy the present, without anxious
dependence upon the future, not to amuse ourselves with
either hopes or fears but to rest satisfied with what we
have, which is sufficient, for he that is so wants nothing.
The greatest blessings of mankind are within us and within
our reach. A wise man is content with his lot, whatever
it may be, without wishing for what he has not.

–Seneca

— 24 —
UNFAILING LOVE

Let them give thanks to the Lord for his unfailing love
and his wonderful deeds for mankind,
for he satisfies the thirsty
and fills the hungry with good things.

–Psalm 107:8-9

— 25 —

DO WHAT IS GOOD FOR EVERYONE

Make sure that nobody pays back wrong for wrong, but always
strive to do what is good for each other and for everyone else.
Rejoice always, pray continually, give thanks in all circumstances;
for this is God's will for you in Christ Jesus. Do not quench
the Spirit. Do not treat prophecies with contempt but test
them all; hold on to what is good, reject every kind of evil.
—1 Thessalonians 5:15–22

— 26 —

COUNT YOUR BLESSINGS. ALWAYS.

We tend to forget
that happiness doesn't come
as a result of getting something we don't have,
but rather of recognizing and appreciating what we do have.
—**Frederick Keonig**

— 27 —

THE GRASS IS NOT GREENER ON THE OTHER SIDE

Do not spoil what you have by desiring what you
have not; remember that what you now have was
once among the things you only hoped for.

–Epicurus

— 28 —

LIVE LIFE TO THE FULLEST

As you keep your mind and heart focused in the right
direction, approaching each day with faith and gratitude,
I believe you will be empowered to live life to the fullest
and enjoy the abundant life He has promised you.

–Victoria Osteen

— 29 —

STAY ON THE BRIGHT SIDE OF LIFE

Let me encourage you to get up every day
and focus on what you do have in life.
Be thankful for the blessings of the little things
even when you don't get what you expect.

–Victoria Osteen

– 30 –

ACCEPTANCE IS WISDOM

Being grateful does not mean that everything is necessarily good.
It just means that you can accept it as a gift.

—Roy T. Bennett

"If we could see the miracle of a single flower
clearly, our whole life would change."
—*Buddha*

"I am content; that is a blessing greater than riches;
and he to whom that is given need ask no more."
—*Henry Fielding*

"Dwell on the beauty of life. Watch the stars,
and see yourself running with them."
—*Marcus Aurelius*

"Hello, sun in my face.
Hello you who made the morning and
spread it over the fields.
...Watch, now, how I start the day
in happiness, in kindness."
—*Mary Oliver, from "Why I Wake Early," Devotions*

"I would maintain that thanks are the
highest form of thought; and that gratitude
is happiness doubled by wonder."
—*G.K. Chesterton*

"When we give cheerfully and accept gratefully,
everyone is blessed."
—*Maya Angelou*

PRAYERFUL PRACTICE: HOW YOU CAN HAVE AN ATTITUDE OF GRATITUDE

1. Be grateful and recognize the things others have done to help you.

2. When you say, "Thank you," to someone, it signals what you appreciate and why you appreciate it.

3. Post a "Thank you to all" on your Facebook page or your blog, or send individual emails to friends, family, and colleagues.

4. Send a handwritten thank-you note. These are noteworthy because so few of us take time to write and mail them.

5. Think thoughts of gratitude—two or three good things that happened today—and notice calm settle through your head, at least for a moment. It activates a part of the brain that floods the body with endorphins, or feel-good hormones.

6. Remember the ways your life has been made easier or better because of others' efforts. Be aware of and acknowledge the good things, large and small, going on around you.

7. Keep a gratitude journal or set aside time each day or evening to list the people or things you're grateful for

today. The list may start out short, but it will grow as you notice more of the good things around you.

8. Being grateful shakes you out of self-absorption and helps you recognize those who've done wonderful things for you. Expressing that gratitude continues to draw those people into your sphere.

9. Remember this thought from Maya Angelou: "When you learn, teach; when you get, give."

10. Join forces to do good. If you have survived illness or loss, you may want to reach out to others to help as a way of showing gratitude for those who reached out to you.

DECEMBER

COMFORT AND JOY: LOOKING AHEAD TO A NEW YEAR RESET

"Now and then it's good to pause in our pursuit of happiness and just be happy."
  —*Guillaume Apollinaire*

"Peace I leave with you, my peace I give unto you: not as the word giveth, give I unto you. Let your heart be troubled, neither let it be afraid."
  —*John 14:278*

"Action may not always bring happiness; but there is no happiness without action."
  —*Benjamin Disraeli*

"Difficult roads often lead to beautiful destinations. The best is yet to come."
  —*Zig Ziglar*

"The two most important days in your life are the day you are born and the day you find out why."
  —*Mark Twain*

252

"If you have easy self-contentment, you might have a very, very cheap source of happiness."
  —*Leon Kass*

— 1 —

LAUGH AS MUCH AS YOU CAN

To laugh often and much; to win the respect of the intelligent
people and the affection of children; to earn the appreciation
of honest critics and endure the betrayal of false friends; to
appreciate beauty; to find the beauty in others; to leave the
world a bit better whether by a healthy child, a garden patch, or
a redeemed social condition; to know that one life has breathed
easier because you lived here. This is to have succeeded.

–Ralph Waldo Emerson

— 2 —

HEAVEN IS HERE, NOW

There is no such thing as hell except
forgetting that heaven is here, now.

We forget so easily. don't we?
life on earth can be so painful.

In our lives that are just as short as they are long,
just as precious as they are strong,
please help us to remember.
that you love us all.

–Anonymous

253

— 3 —

RIVERS OF HAPPINESS

May the winds bring us happiness.
May the rivers carry happiness to us.
May the plants give us happiness.
May night and day yield us happiness.
May the dust of the earth bring us happiness.
May the heavens give us happiness.
May the trees give us happiness.
May the sun pour down happiness.

I offer my salutations to the
Supreme Being, the all-pervading Spirit.
—Taittirya Aranyaka

— 4 —

MOTHER EARTH'S WINTER

As days grow dark our thoughts go too
We're motionless in the cold
Now is the time to stop and rest
Give thought to what we hold
We're created in Her image
How can we feel forlorn?

Let go of waste and empty want
Become Her child once more!
–Anonymous

— 5 —

LET EVERY VOICE BE HEARD

May those without voice be heard.
May those without food be fed.
May those who are harmed be healed.
May the earth's health be restored.
May all have peace, equality, inclusion for all.
–Alycia Longriver Davis

— 6 —

THE COURAGE TO SERVE OTHERS

Show me the suffering of the most miserable;
So I will know my people's plight.

Free me to pray for others;
For you are present in every person.

Help me take responsibility for my own life;
So that I can be free at last.

Grant me courage to serve others;
For in service there is true life.

Give me honesty and patience;
So that the Spirit will be alive among us.

Let the Spirit flourish and grow;
So that we will never tire of the struggle.

Let us remember those who have died for justice;
For they have given us life.

Help us love even those who hate us;
So we can change the world.

Amen.

−**César E. Chávez**

− 7 −

GOODNESS AND LOVE

The Lord is my shepherd, I lack nothing. He makes me lie down in green pastures, he leads me beside quiet waters, he refreshes my soul. He guides me along the right paths for his name's sake. Even though I walk through the darkest valley, I will fear no evil, for you are with me; your rod and your staff, they comfort me. You prepare a table before me in the presence of my enemies. You anoint my head with oil; my cup overflows. Surely your goodness and love will follow me all the days of my life and I will dwell in the house of the Lord forever.

−Psalm 23:1-6

256

— 8 —

REMEMBER

Remember the sky that you were born under,
know each of the star's stories.
Remember the moon, know who she is.
Remember the sun's birth at dawn, that is the
strongest point of time. Remember sundown
and the giving away to night.
Remember your birth, how your mother struggled
to give you form and breath. You are evidence of
her life, and her mother's, and hers.
Remember your father. He is your life, also.
Remember the earth whose skin you are:
red earth, black earth, yellow earth, white earth
brown earth, we are earth.
Remember the plants, trees, animal life who all have their
tribes, their families, their histories, too. Talk to them,
listen to them. They are alive poems.
Remember the wind. Remember her voice. She knows the
origin of this universe.
Remember you are all people and all people
are you.
Remember you are this universe and this
universe is you.
Remember all is in motion, is growing, is you.
Remember language comes from this.
Remember the dance language is, that life is.
Remember.

—Joy Harjo

— 9 —

THE KEY

Learn to let go. That is the key to happiness.
—Buddha

— 10 —

THIS NEW DAY

This new day is too dear,
with its hopes and invitations,
to waste a moment on the rotten yesterdays.
—Ralph Waldo Emerson

— 11 —

MAKE A LITTLE MUSIC WITH YOUR HEART

When the song of the angels is stilled,
when the star in the sky is gone,
when the kings and princes are home,
when the shepherds are back with the flocks,
then the work of Christmas begins:
To find the lost, to heal those broken in spirit,
to feed the hungry, to release the oppressed,
to rebuild the nations, to bring peace among all peoples,
to make a little music with the heart.

And to radiate the Light of Christ, every day,
in every way, in all that we do and in all that we say.
Then the work of Christmas begins.

–Howard Thurman

— 12 —

IN STILLNESS, YOU CAN HEAR GOD

I speak to you. Be still
Know I am God.
I spoke to you when you were born. Be still
Know I am God.
I spoke to you at your first sight. Be still
Know I am God.
I spoke to you at your first word. Be still
Know I am God.
I spoke to you at your first thought. Be still
Know I am God.
I spoke to you at your first love. Be still
Know I am God.
I spoke to you at your first song. Be still
Know I am God.

–Essene Gospel of Peace

— 13 —

EVERYTHING IS BEAUTIFUL

Every day I feel is a blessing from God.
And I consider it a new beginning.
Yeah, everything is beautiful.

—Prince

— 14 —

LOOK TO TOMORROW

With the new day comes new strength and new thoughts.

—Eleanor Roosevelt

— 15 —

JUST LET IT GO

Renew, release, let go.
Yesterday's gone.
There's nothing you can do to bring it back.
You can't "should've" done something.
You can only do something
Renew yourself.
Release that attachment.
Today is a new day!

—Steve Maraboli

— 16 —

CATCH THE TRADE WIND IN YOUR SAILS

Twenty years from now
you will be more disappointed
by the things that you didn't do
than by the ones you did do.
So throw off the bowlines.
Sail away from the safe harbor.
Catch the trade winds in your sails.
Explore. Dream. Discover.
–H. Jackson Brown Jr.

— 17 —

WHEREVER YOU GO, THERE YOU ARE

All the suffering,
stress,
and addiction
comes from not realizing
you already are what you are looking for.
–Jon Kabat-Zinn

261

— 18 —

SEND THOSE WORRIES AWAY

You know, people just assume,
"Well, all my life I'll be a worrier."
That doesn't have to be true.
There's a way to drink
from God's presence so much
that worry begins to dissipate.
—Max Lucado

— 19 —

HINDSIGHT REALLY IS 20/20

When I look back on all these worries,
I remember the story of the old man
who said on his deathbed
that he had a lot of trouble in his life,
most of which never happened.
—Winston Churchill

— 20 —

LIVE LONG AND PROSPER

May the whole world enjoy
good health,
long life,
prosperity,

happiness and peace.
Om, shanti, shanti, shanti.
–Vethathiri Maharishi

— 21 —

YOLO!

Dance as though no one is watching you,
Love as though you have never been hurt before,
Sing as though no one can hear you,
Live as though heaven is on earth.
–Susanna Clark and Richard Leigh

— 22 —

THE BOOK OF LIFE

Blessings, O sweet blessings,
to you who listened to me
whenever I was troubled, raging mad or sad,
whenever I needed to release
the feelings that had bound me
to dusty corners, narrow spaces, cloudy skies.
Gratitude, my sweet ones,
gratitude and blessings
to you for the time you took
to see my tenderness and sorrows

263

with eyes of love–
and with the certainty that God
would wipe away my tears
were I to allow myself to cry in deepest prayer.
Blessings, O sweet blessings
be upon you, my dear friends,
for trusting in the bonds that tie
moon and sun together, the bonds
uniting us, one soul to another,
during the final hours of the day
when we give the book of life
to God for his safekeeping,
when we ask God and stars to watch over us
through the dark and holy night of our *tikkun*.
–Elliott Robertson

— 23 —

BLESSING OF THE EARTH

It is lovely indeed, it is lovely indeed.
I, I am the spirit within the earth...
The feet of the earth are my feet...
The legs of the earth are my legs...
The bodily strength of the earth is my strength...
The thoughts of the earth are my thoughts...
The voice of the earth is my voice...
The feather of the earth is my feather...
All that belongs to the earth belongs to me...

264

All that surrounds the earth surrounds me...
I, I am the sacred words of the earth...
It is lovely indeed, it is lovely indeed.
—Navajo Song

— 24 —

CUP OF PRAYER

Beloved, to Thee I raise my whole being,
a vessel emptied of self. Accept, O Lord,
this my emptiness, and so fill me with
Thy Self—Thy Light, Thy Love, Thy
Life—that these Thy precious Gifts
may radiate through me and over-
flow the chalice of my heart into
the hearts of all with whom I
come in contact this day,
revealing unto them
the beauty of
Thy joy
and
Wholeness
and
the
serenity
of Thy Peace
which nothing can destroy.
—Francis Nuttall

— 25 —

JOYOUS JOURNEYS

May the long time sun
Shine upon you,
All love surround you,
And the pure light within you
Guide your way on.
—Mike Heron of the Incredible String Band

— 26 —

MANTRA FOR ANXIETY

This is not you.
This is something moving through you.
It can leave out of the same door it came in.
—Cleo Wade

— 27 —

LIKE GREEN GRASS GROWING

Now the green blade rises
from the buried grain,
Wheat that in the dark earth
many years has lain;
Love lives again, that

with the dead has been:

Love is come again, like
wheat that springs up green.

In the grave they laid Him,
Love Whom we had slain,
Thinking that He'd never
wake to life again,
Laid in the earth like
grain that sleeps unseen:

Love is come again, like
wheat that springs up green.

When our hearts are saddened,
grieving or in pain,
By Your touch You call us
back to life again;
Fields of our hearts that
dead and bare have been:

Love is come again, like
wheat that springs up green.
–John Macleod Campbell Crum

– 28 –

ACTS OF LOVE

This new Bible shall be written
On the hearts of all mankind,

Not by pen or book,
But by acts of Love.
For to Love as She does
Is to truly know who He is.
The unchanged truth is eternal life
For all, without exception.
For no longer do we wander lost in the Word,
But live the word in eternal life.
—Justina M. Pernetter

— 29 —
THE LONG VIEW

It helps, now and then, to step back and take a long view.
The kingdom is not only beyond our efforts,
it is even beyond our vision.
We accomplish in our lifetime only a tiny fraction
of the magnificent enterprise that is God's work.

Nothing we do is complete, which is a way of
saying that the Kingdom always lies beyond us.
No statement says all that could be said.
No prayer fully expresses our faith.
No confession brings perfection.
No pastoral visit brings wholeness.
No program accomplishes the Church's mission.
No set of goals and objectives includes everything.

This is what we are about. We plant the
seeds that one day will grow.
We water seeds already planted, knowing
that they hold future promise.
We lay foundations that will need further development.
We provide yeast that produces far beyond our capabilities.

We cannot do everything, and there is a
sense of liberation in realizing that.
This enables us to do something, and to do it very well.
It may be incomplete, but it is a beginning, a step along the way,
an opportunity for the Lord's grace to enter and do the rest.

We may never see the end results, but that is the difference
between the master builder and the worker.
We are workers, not master builders; ministers, not messiahs.
We are prophets of a future not our own.

–**Bishop Ken Untener**

— 30 —

BRUSHING TROUBLES OFF

May your walking be easy, on dry land or snow.
May the good Lord walk with you wherever you go.
May your troubles brush off, like a sprinkling of dust,
And may you stand strong, for what is good, what is just.

269

May your soul be always grateful, may joy fill your heart.
May you reach out to others, with love, from the start.
May friendships bring blessing for you every day.
And may you be a blessing to those on your way.
—Reverend Jane R. Dunning

— 31 —

A NEW START

Let there be respect for the earth,
Peace for its people,
Love in our lives,
Delight in the good,
Forgiveness for past wrongs
And from now on, a new start.
—Reverend Peter Trow

CARE FOR THE SOUL

"Trust yourself. You've survived a lot, and
you'll survive whatever is coming."

—*Robert Tew*

"Which of you by worrying can add
one cubit to his stature?"

—*Matthew 6:27*

"Worrying doesn't empty tomorrow of its
sorrow, it empties today of its strength."

—*Corrie ten Boom*

"Keep walking through the storm. Your
rainbow is waiting on the other side."

—*Heather Stillufsen*

"Fear and anxiety many times indicate that we are moving
in a positive direction, out of the safe confines of our
comfort zone, and in the direction of our true purpose."

—*Charles F. Glassman*

"Every sunset is an opportunity to reset."

—*Richie Norton*

PRAYERFUL PRACTICE: CREATING A PRAYER CIRCLE

In closing, I want to share with you one last way that you can express all of this newfound calm, and that is by creating a "Prayer and Blessings Circle." The idea is simple. A gratitude circle is a place for counting blessings and sharing stories, photos, prayers of serenity, and videos with friends and loved ones. The more people you can get to align with you, the sooner you will discover the positive power of gratitude and reap the many benefits that come from doing so. Now, we want to spread that gift and help you become cheerleaders for others who have tapped into the power of thankfulness by forming your own Prayer Circle. Connect with others in this special group that's dedicated to honoring the simple phrases, "Thank you" and "I am grateful for..." We know firsthand that once you start a thankfulness circle, it won't take long for others to join in, and the power of gratefulness will permeate and bless your everyday being. Here are my tips for starting a circle.

1. **Organize.** As the organizer, consider yourself the host or hostess, almost as if you have invited a group of friends—or people you hope will become friends—to your dinner table. Your role is to help guide conversations and serve up a feast (of interesting stories about gratitude or nuggets of information to

share) that will keep the conversations meaningful, inspiring, and ultimately bring to life the power of gratitude in all the lives of those gathered in your circle.

2. **Create a Mission or Goals for Your Circle.** What do you want to accomplish? How will you manifest gratitude in your own life and the lives of those in your circle? Will you share stories, inspiring quotes, guided meditations? Create a plan for guiding your group through the practice of gratitude.

3. **Decide Whether to Meet Online or In Person.** The exciting thing about the Internet is that you can create a Circle and community online and connect friends and colleagues from across the country—and the world. Or you may want to create an in-person circle with friends in your neighborhood or town.

4. **Make Connections.** Send out evites and invites and make phone calls to invite members to your circle. Ask everyone to invite a friend and spread the word about your new group.

5. **Select a Meet-Up Place.** Often guides will invite in-person communities to meet at their home. Or you may opt for a local coffee shop or a comfortable meeting place where you can gather regularly.

273

6. **Schedule.** Create a calendar of meet-up dates and distribute it to your group.

7. **Create Materials.** In this book we have lots of prompts and prayers as well as meditations and exercises to try. Please feel free to tap into these as resources.

8. **Talk About It.** Spread the good news about what being thankful can do as it manifests in your life and the lives of your friends, family, and members of your circle.

Circles of Grace

Those simple suggestions should help you and your circle get started. Remember, nothing is cast in stone, and you can feel free to improvise until you find your comfort zone. We guarantee you will come away from these gatherings feeling inspired, challenged, and with exciting new ideas to share.

First, begin by welcoming your guests. Go around the circle with each person introducing themselves; for example, "I am Mary Smith and I live in Ohio. I am a writer, literacy volunteer, and mother of two." Next, read a passage of poetry, prayer, or prose. Now, go clockwise around the circle, and ask each participant why she or he is here and what spiritual sustenance he or she is seeking.

Ask a volunteer to read her favorite prayer or quote about being thankful. These group gatherings are wonderful, but personal sharing and goal discussion can be intimidating at first, so be mindful of your group and you'll sense when you will need to wrap things up. Always end on a high note by asking each person to share gratitude. May your transformation be your inspiration!

ABOUT THE AUTHOR

Becca Anderson comes from a long line of preachers and teachers from Ohio and Kentucky. The teacher side of her family led her to become a woman's studies scholar and the author of *The Book of Awesome Women*. An avid collector of meditations, prayers, and blessings, she helps run a "Gratitude and Grace Circle" that meets monthly at homes, churches, and bookstores in the San Francisco Bay Area, where she currently resides. Becca Anderson credits her spiritual practice with helping her recover from cancer and wants to share this with anyone who is facing difficulty in their life.

Author of *Think Happy to Stay Happy* and *Every Day Thankful*, Becca Anderson shares her inspirational writings and suggested acts of kindness at thedailyinspoblog. wordpress.com.

Mango Publishing, established in 2014, publishes an eclectic list of books by diverse authors—both new and established voices— on topics ranging from business, personal growth, women's empowerment, LGBTQ studies, health, and spirituality to history, popular culture, time management, decluttering, lifestyle, mental wellness, aging, and sustainable living. We were recently named 2019's #1 fastest growing independent publisher by *Publishers Weekly*. Our success is driven by our main goal, which is to publish high quality books that will entertain readers as well as make a positive difference in their lives.

Our readers are our most important resource; we value your input, suggestions, and ideas. We'd love to hear from you—after all, we are publishing books for you!

Please stay in touch with us and follow us at:

Facebook: Mango Publishing
Twitter: @MangoPublishing
Instagram: @MangoPublishing
LinkedIn: Mango Publishing
Pinterest: Mango Publishing

Sign up for our newsletter at www.mangopublishinggroup.com and receive a free book!

Join us on Mango's journey to reinvent publishing, one book at a time.